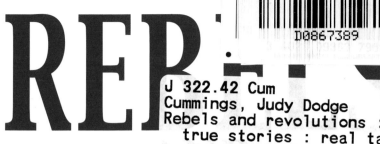

REB~~ELS~~

AND

REVOLUTIONS

TRUE STORIES

Real Tales of Radical Change in America

JUDY DODGE CUMMINGS

Nomad Press
A division of Nomad Communications
10 9 8 7 6 5 4 3 2 1

This book was manufactured by CGB Printers,
North Mankato, Minnesota, United States
August 2017, Job #228807
ISBN Softcover: 978-1-61930-551-9
ISBN Hardcover: 978-1-61930-547-2

Educational Consultant, Marla Conn

Questions regarding the ordering of this book should be addressed to
Nomad Press
2456 Christian St.
White River Junction, VT 05001
www.nomadpress.net

Printed in the United States.

Contents

Titles in the
Mystery & Mayhem Series

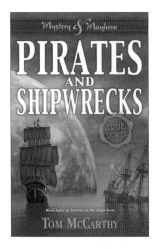

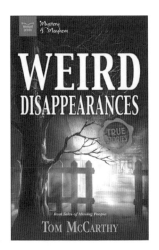

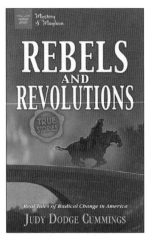

Check out more titles at www.nomadpress.net

Introduction
Are You a Rule Breaker?

Have you ever been ordered to do something
that was unfair? Such as clean up a mess
you did not make or let someone go who
rudely cut the line when you'd patiently
waited for your turn? Most people encounter
unfairness sometime in their lives.

What if you were commanded to follow a rule that
made you feel like a criminal every day, year in and
year out? Disobeying the rule could get you jailed
or killed. Would you swallow your pride and follow
orders or stand up for your rights, regardless of the
consequences?

History is full of people who have been labeled
troublemakers because they rebelled against rules
they believed were unjust. This book tells the stories
of five real-life rule breakers.

Joseph Plumb Martin was only 15 when he stood up to the king of England. Joseph joined the Continental Army to help the American colonies fight for independence.

When he picked up a musket and vowed to overthrow British rule in America, Joseph became a traitor. If captured, he would be imprisoned and possibly executed.

Joseph Plumb Martin fought for his country's freedom, but Sengbe Pieh fought for his personal freedom. Kidnapped by slave traders in Africa, Sengbe was shackled in the hold of a slave ship headed for America. He broke free from his chains and led fellow captives in a revolt against the ship's crew. The Africans commandeered the ship and tried to sail back to Africa, but the U.S. Navy captured them. Sengbe was imprisoned on murder charges.

Members of the Fair Play Committee knew what it meant to lose freedom. When the United States went to war with Japan in 1941, the government moved 120,000 people of Japanese ancestry into internment camps. The majority of these people were American citizens. Their "crime?" A Japanese heritage. In 1944, the government began drafting the men held in the camps to fight in the war.

A group that called itself the Fair Play Committee refused to go along with the draft until families were released from the camps. Fair Play Committee members wanted their families to be allowed to go home. The government refused, and charged members of the group with treason.

Claudette Colvin did not live behind bars, but she did live in a kind of prison. As a black teenager growing up in Alabama in the 1950s, racist laws restricted her life in many miserable ways. One day, Claudette's tolerance for these rules ran out. She refused to give up her seat on the bus to a white woman. Claudette was arrested.

Cesar Chavez also lived with the injustices of racial discrimination. A Mexican-American migrant worker, he toiled in the fields of California. Long hours, low wages, and brutal conditions kept his family and other farm laborers in poverty. Cesar became the voice of these workers. He stood up to the agricultural industry and demanded better working conditions for the people who labor to pick the nation's fruits and vegetables.

These five individuals fought for their rights and changed history. Their stories might inspire you to become a rebel for the right cause.

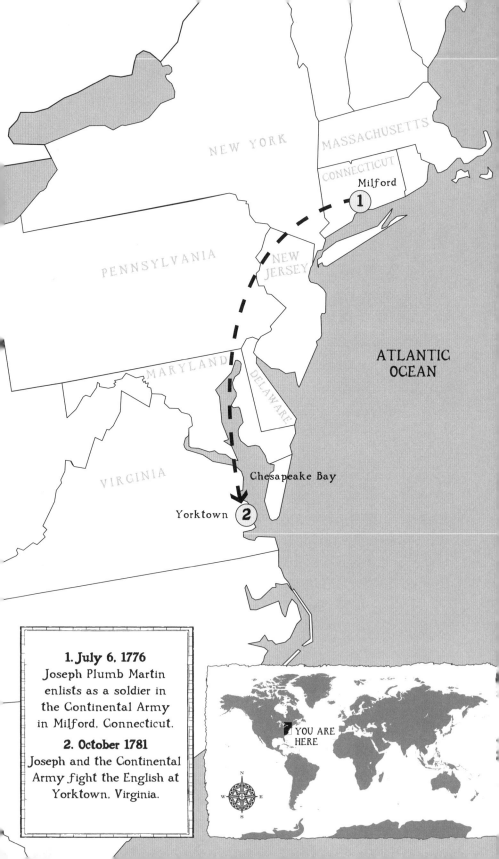

NEW YORK

MASSACHUSETTS

CONNECTICUT

Milford

①

PENNSYLVANIA

NEW JERSEY

MARYLAND

DELAWARE

ATLANTIC OCEAN

VIRGINIA

Chesapeake Bay

Yorktown ②

1. July 6, 1776
Joseph Plumb Martin
enlists as a soldier in
the Continental Army
in Milford, Connecticut.

2. October 1781
Joseph and the Continental
Army fight the English at
Yorktown, Virginia.

YOU ARE HERE

N
W   E
S

1770	1776	1783
◆———————————————	——————◆————————	—————————◆
Boston Massacre	The Declaration of Independence	The Revolutionary War ends

Chapter One

Soldier of the Revolution

The morning of April 21, 1775, church
bells clanged in the small town of Milford,
Connecticut, followed by three rapid gunshots.

Joseph Plumb Martin, who was 15 years old, put down his plow and looked at his grandfather in alarm. "I smell a rat," Grandfather said. Without another word, he steered the horse cart for home.

Joseph sniffed.

That was no rat he smelled. It was war.

This is the true tale of Joseph Plumb Martin, a boy who rebelled against the greatest power in the world of the eighteenth century—the British Empire. He did it in defense of his country and his brothers-in-arms.

Joseph Plumb Martin was born in 1760 in Becket, Massachusetts. His father was a pastor who frequently moved. When Joseph was seven, his parents sent him to live with his grandparents on their farm outside Milford, Connecticut.

During the 1760s, the American colonies began to resist trade restrictions placed on them by their mother country, Great Britain. When the British Parliament taxed molasses imports, the colonists smuggled in barrels of the syrupy stuff instead of paying the extra fee. When Great Britain required newspapers and playing cards to be printed on paper that was taxed, Americans boycotted these goods.

As Joseph grew older, the chasm between Great Britain and America grew deeper.

The colonists objected to the arrival of British troops in Boston, Massachusetts, in 1768, sent by the king of England to maintain order. During a chaotic protest on March 5, 1770, British soldiers shot and killed five colonists in an incident named the Boston Massacre.

Tensions simmered as the months passed. On the evening of December 16, 1773, more than 100 colonists climbed aboard three British ships moored in Boston Harbor. The colonists destroyed 340 chests of tea. They tossed 92,000 pounds of the stuff into the sea to protest the British tax on tea.

Joseph was only 13, but he understood a line had been crossed. Outrage swept across Britain. Parliament closed down Boston Harbor and banned town meetings throughout New England. People in Milford began to speak of war.

This talk made Joseph nervous. He was convinced he must be a coward. "What," he wrote years later, "venture my carcass where bullets fly! That will never do for me." But his attitude changed that morning in 1775 when the church bells pealed. Joseph did not follow Grandfather home. Instead, he headed to the village.

The boys and men of the community were gathered at Clark's Tavern, their blood running high. Joseph soon learned why. On April 19, British troops had fired on colonial militia in Lexington, Massachusetts. Called Redcoats, the British soldiers killed eight men. Later that day, American militia and the Redcoats battled in nearby Concord and more men died on both sides.

War was no longer a rumor.

At Clark's Tavern, men were being paid to enlist in the Continental Army to defend the American colonies from the British. New recruits would head out in just days.

The sight of the money caused "seeds of courage to sprout" in Joseph. But he was too young to enlist without his grandfather's permission.

Grandfather refused to give it, and Joseph sank into a glum silence.

The morning the recruits left Milford, Joseph marched with them to the town line. Some of his friends had enlisted and envy filled Joseph's heart.

When the fighting ended, these buddies would swagger back to town, bragging about all their "hairbreadth escapes." Joseph would have no stories to tell. "O," he thought, "that was too much to be borne by me."

Days passed. Joseph tilled the same fields and milked the same cows. Each day was just like the one before. Joseph considered enlisting without his grandfather's permission, but just could not do it. His grandparents had always been kind and generous. But if they ever did something really unfair, Joseph decided, he would enlist in the army in a heartbeat, without a speck of guilt.

Although he knew it was rotten, Joseph began to pray that his grandparents would wrong him in some way. In the fall, Joseph's prayers were answered.

One thing Joseph loved was his grandfather's "playdays." After weeks of hard work during spring planting and fall harvesting, Joseph was allowed a full day with no work. In the fall of 1775, Grandfather said that as soon as the winter grain crop was planted, Joseph could have a playday. Joseph wanted to attend a graduation ceremony in nearby New Haven.

"You shall go," Grandfather promised. "You shall have your choice of our horses to ride there, and I will give you some pocket money."

Joseph and his friends concocted "a thousand and one plans" for the fun they would have.

Two days before the graduation, Grandfather sent Joseph to rake hay in a nearby salt marsh. These swampy grasslands are created when silt washes over coastal lowlands. Farmers cut the salt marsh hay with scythes, and once it dried, they raked it into haycocks. These rounded piles protected the grass from moisture until it could be carted away.

On graduation day, Joseph woke early but Grandfather was not there. Joseph could not leave without his permission, so he paced the kitchen impatiently.

Finally, Grandfather returned. "Come, get up the team," he said before Joseph could say a word. "I've hired the neighbor boy. Today, the three of us are going to haul the hay home from the salt marsh."

Joseph would never refuse an order from his grandfather, nor backtalk him. Still, Joseph was determined to let Grandfather know how angry and hurt he was at this betrayal.

Joseph harnessed the horses to the cart, but he did not climb beside Grandfather. Instead, he walked to the salt marsh. On the way, he saw his friends who were headed to New Haven for the graduation.

"Your grandsire never intended to let you go, and you was a fool to believe him," one boy said.

As his buddies headed off for their day of fun, Joseph stewed.

By midafternoon, Grandfather, the hired boy, and Joseph had loaded the wagon. But more hay stood in the lower marsh. This swampy section was no place to drive a horse team once dusk fell. Grandfather might accidentally steer the horses into a bog. If a horse sank, it could break a leg.

"I'll drive the team home and unload the cart," Grandfather said. "You boys move the rest of the hay off the marsh to the high ground. Have it ready when I return."

With Grandfather gone, the rebellion that had been smoldering inside Joseph all morning burst into flame. "Now [is] the time for me to show my spunk," he thought.

Apple trees, heavy with ripe fruit, grew on the hillside above the marsh. Joseph picked some and stretched out on the ground under the shade of a tree. The hired boy joined him. But as the minutes ticked by, the boy grew nervous.

"We'd best get to work," the boy said.

Joseph took another chomp from his apple.

After much begging, the hired boy finally talked Joseph down to the lower marsh. But there was no fire in Joseph's limbs on this afternoon. The boys had only removed one haycock from the field when Grandfather returned with the cart.

The old man was livid. "Who is to blame?" Grandfather demanded.

Joseph folded his arms across his chest and said nothing.

The hired boy pointed at Joseph. Grandfather grabbed the 6-foot whip he used on the horses and flew at his grandson. Joseph ran.

Other people haying that day watched the scene. Joseph ran at top speed, dodging behind trees and leaping over bushes. The old man clambered after him, whip in hand, face as red as a tomato. But Joseph was far too nimble for Grandfather to catch. The crowd burst into laughter.

Embarrassed, Grandfather gave up and returned to the cart. Perhaps spurred on by fury, Grandfather threw caution to the wind and drove the cart onto the marsh. Joseph returned and helped fill the wagon, but remained out of Grandfather's reach.

As weeks went by, Joseph nursed his anger over being denied his playday. Grandfather's broken promise would be Joseph's "passport into the army."

Following the bloodshed in Lexington and Concord, leaders from the 13 colonies had formed the Second Continental Congress. Throughout the summer and fall of 1775, they debated the future of America. Some leaders wanted to make peace with Great Britain, while others wanted the colonies to declare independence.

As Joseph listened to neighbors talk about the possibility of full-scale war with Great Britain, patriotism surged inside him. Joseph was anxious to "be called a defender of my country."

In June 1776, recruiters for the Continental Army returned to Milford to enlist soldiers for six-month stints. Joseph went to Clark's Tavern every night. He watched men enroll, but always chickened out at the last minute.

One night, his friends started teasing him.

"If you enlist, I will," said one boy. "You've long been talking about it," said another. "Now is the time."

Joseph sat down at the table, and the officer handed him the enlistment forms. As a friend leaned over his shoulder, Joseph held his hand over the form and scribbled his name in the air, careful not to touch the pen to the paper. He was still afraid of taking that final step.

Then, the boy behind him nudged Joseph's arm. The pen scratched across the enrollment form. "O, he has enlisted," said the boy. "He has made his mark."

Joseph shrugged. The time for hesitation was over. He signed and dated the form properly.

July 6, 1776.

Joseph Plumb Martin

Third Company of the Fifth Battalion.

At breakfast the next morning, Joseph tried to work up the courage to break the news to his grandparents. Before he could do it, Grandfather said, "Well, you are going a soldiering then, are you?"

Although Grandfather had not wanted Joseph to join the army, he gave his grandson everything a soldier needed in 1776. This included a musket, cartridge box, haversack filled with extra clothing, silverware, plate and cup, tinderbox, razor, comb, and fishhook and twine. Joseph's grandmother also put in "cake, and cheese in plenty . . . [and] my pocket Bible . . . ."

Joseph knew his grandparents "wished me well, soul and body." His rebellion against Grandfather was over. But his resistance against the British was just beginning.

In July 1776, thousands of British troops landed on Staten Island, New York, within striking distance of the vital port of New York City. Joseph's regiment headed to New York City along with the rest of the Continental Army.

At 6 p.m. on July 9, 1776, thousands of Continental soldiers marched to the parade grounds at the commons in Lower Manhattan. General George Washington announced the news. Days earlier, the Continental Congress had declared the "United Colonies of North America to be free and independent states." Washington ordered the Declaration of Independence be read aloud to the troops.

Every soldier gathered on that commons was now committed to a full-scale revolution.

It was victory or death.

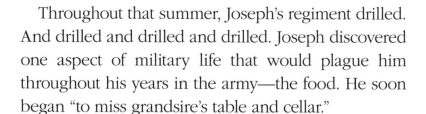

Throughout that summer, Joseph's regiment drilled. And drilled and drilled and drilled. Joseph discovered one aspect of military life that would plague him throughout his years in the army—the food. He soon began "to miss grandsire's table and cellar."

Meanwhile, the British forces on Staten Island swelled. By mid-August, British General William Howe commanded 30 warships, 400 boats, 32,000 soldiers, and 10,000 sailors. Not sure where the British would strike, General Washington divided his 20,000 troops between Manhattan itself and Brooklyn, the section of Long Island that lay across the East River from Manhattan.

When British troops landed on Long Island on August 22, their target was clear. A large hill known as the Heights runs down the spine of Brooklyn. Washington fortified the hill and concentrated 3,000 soldiers on three roads that led to this high ground. However, the general made a nearly fatal mistake.

A little-known and rarely used trail called Jamaica Pass also led to the Heights. British scouts discovered a gap here in the American defenses, and General Howe laid a trap that could have ended the war.

On August 26, under the cover of darkness, 10,000 British soldiers silently crept up Jamaica Pass. To divert the Americans from this rear assault, nine British warships sailed straight for Manhattan. General Howe ordered two simultaneous attacks against the bulk of the American defenses on the Heights.

All of the American commanders, including General Washington, were caught by surprise when thousands of Redcoats hit them from behind.

When Joseph and his regiment reached Brooklyn, he confronted the horrors of battle face to face. The wounded and dead lay strewn across the plain, "some with broken arms, some with broken legs, and some with broken heads."

Joseph's regiment fought a series of skirmishes with the British. They raced through cornfields and woods, dodging musket balls. The men slept on the ground as rain poured down, the growling of their bellies rivaling the boom of thunder. After two nights of this, Joseph went to a nearby barn to get dry straw to lie on. The sun was setting when he returned to camp, only to discover the entire regiment marching away. Joseph grabbed his gear and fell into formation.

As the men marched, an order came down the lines—absolutely no talking. Wagon wheels were muffled with cloth. Rain sluiced down Joseph's hat as he marched in silence with no idea where he was going.

General Washington knew the British encircled the Continental Army. The morning would bring slaughter or surrender. The only escape route lay across the East River to Manhattan.

The army marched in silent double-time to a ferry landing. Battling rough waves and twisting currents, a company of Massachusetts fishermen rowed the army across the river, one boatload at a time. Joseph's feet touched Manhattan at 3 in the morning.

Many Americans still waited on the banks of Long Island. When dawn broke, the British would spot these troops and capture or kill them.

Before the sun rose, fog thick as pea soup descended over the harbor. Hidden by the mist, the entire Continental Army escaped. When the fog cleared, the British discovered their enemy had vanished.

The American rebellion was not over.

On Christmas day of 1776, Joseph received a present. His six-month enlistment had ended. Joseph returned home to enjoy his grandmother's cooking.

However, as spring tiptoed into Connecticut, Joseph grew restless. His country was still not free and he felt a duty to help win its liberty. On April 12, 1777, Joseph reenlisted. This time he would fight for the duration of the war. Little did anyone realize, the war would drag on for six more years. Six more years of hunger, sleeping on the wet ground, and risking life and limb in defense of the United States of America.

Joseph's revolutionary spirit was put to the test many times. In November 1777, he defended Fort Mifflin, an island fortress in the Delaware River, when the British laid siege to it. Joseph said the Americans put up with "hardships sufficient to kill half a dozen horses."

The British bombarded the island until the land resembled a plowed field. The rain of artillery was so constant that Joseph could not sleep for more than a few minutes at a time.

On November 15, American officers decided to abandon the fort. While 300 survivors were rowed across the river to New Jersey, Joseph and a crew of 40 men remained behind to burn the barracks before they evacuated. That night, British ships drew close to the island in preparation for an invasion the next morning.

"We will give it to the damned rebels in the morning," said a British soldier, his voice carrying across the water.

Hunkered inside the barracks, Joseph whispered. "The damned rebels will show you a trick. They will go off and leave you."

After setting fire to the barracks, Joseph and the other Continental soldiers escaped by boat as cannonballs hammered them.

As the war for independence dragged on, Joseph's rebellion transformed. While he still fought the British, he also rose up against his own commanders. It was Joseph's belly, not his patriotic spirit, that spurred on this resistance.

The soldiers were forced to constantly forage for food because the army never provided enough rations. On one excursion, Joseph and friends in his company nabbed a goose from a farmyard. They plucked and roasted it, mouths watering all the while. But when the men divided the goose evenly, Joseph was left with one measly wing to fill his cavern of a belly.

For Thanksgiving dinner in 1777, the troops were supplied with an extra ration of rice and a tablespoonful of vinegar. Joseph and his friends were caught sneaking a few pounds of beef from the camp's storehouse to supplement this "feast," and the meat was taken away from them.

Thanksgiving dinner consisted of "a leg of nothing and no turnips."

Despite this deprivation, Joseph did not lose faith in the American cause. "We had engaged in the defense of our injured country," he recalled, "we were determined to persevere as long as such hardships were not altogether intolerable."

But the hardships did become intolerable during the winter of 1779–1780. For the first time in recorded history, all the bays and inlets along the Atlantic Ocean north of North Carolina froze solid. In early January, 1780, a four-day snowstorm buried the Continental Army's winter camp in Morristown, New Jersey. Food supplies could not be delivered.

Joseph declared the troops were "absolutely, literally starved." The only thing he ate during these four days was a piece of birch bark. Men roasted their old shoes and the officers stewed their pet dog. Men deserted because they couldn't bear the hunger.

Surely rations would improve in spring. But still they received only "musty bread and a little beef, about every other day . . . ." One evening in May 1780, the troops reached their breaking point.

The men had spent the day drilling on empty stomachs and some grew grouchy.

"You're a mutinous rascal," an officer said to one of his sergeants.

The sergeant stamped the butt of his musket on the ground. "Who will parade with me?" he called.

The entire Eighth Regiment fell into formation behind the sergeant. These soldiers were armed and marching in battle formation without the permission of their commanding officers. This was a violation of military law. The threat of the hungry army attacking its own commanders was a powder keg. If someone lit a match, the American Revolution would destroy itself.

The Fourth Regiment had been drilling nearby and they joined the Connecticut Eighth. The troops then decided to locate the two other regiments camped at Morristown and convince them to join their uprising.

In a panic, the officers tried to coax the soldiers to return to their quarters.

"There is good news for you boys," one colonel lied. "A large shipment of cattle has arrived for the army."

The men did not fall for this. But they were hungry, not treasonous. They grumbled a little longer, then eventually returned to their quarters.

"We were unwilling to desert the cause of our country . . . ," Joseph later wrote. Two days after this mutiny, a shipment of pork and cattle arrived in camp. The crisis passed, but the problem of feeding the Continental Army was not solved. A near constant hunger plagued Joseph until his last days as a soldier.

Those last days drew closer with the help of the French. On July 6, 1781, Washington and his French counterpart, Count de Rochambeau, met in rural New York. Each man commanded roughly 4,000 soldiers, and they plotted to retake New York City, which was then occupied by British forces under General Henry Clinton.

A stunning piece of news changed their plans and altered the war.

———◆———

On August 14, French Admiral Francois de Grasse planned to sail from the Caribbean with all the ships and troops he could muster. He would head for Yorktown, Virginia, located on a peninsula in the Chesapeake Bay. About 8,000 Redcoats were camped there under the leadership of British General Charles Cornwallis. De Grasse would blockade the bay so

Cornwallis could neither be resupplied nor evacuated by sea. Armed with this news, Generals Washington and Rochambeau concocted a bold strategy.

A combined American-French army would march from New York to Virginia, a distance of almost 600 miles. This would hem Cornwallis in before he could escape by land.

But they had to move quietly. If General Henry Clinton discovered the enemy was heading south instead of attacking New York, he would send the British fleet to evacuate Cornwallis. Admiral de Grasse needed time to sail from the Caribbean and get his fleet in blockade position in the Chesapeake Bay.

What the American cause needed now was speed, secrecy, and luck.

On August 18, 1781, the American-French army began to march south. Only a few officers knew where the army was headed. The troops were divided into three columns to better hide from any British scouts working for General Clinton.

Joseph sailed south instead of marching. He had been promoted to the Sapper and Miner Corps. This group was responsible for laying out the army's camps and building roads and fortifications. He arrived in Yorktown on September 28 and went to work.

The British had constructed a line of defense around Yorktown made up of 10 small forts called redoubts.

The Sapper and Miner Corps had to dig a trench 800 yards from this line of redoubts. By October 9, the trench was finished and the attack began.

For 48 hours, the Americans and French bombarded Yorktown, destroying most of the British artillery and eight redoubts. Joseph was ordered back on duty to dig a second trench, this time 400 yards from British fortifications. However, redoubts nine and ten stood in the way of this second trench.

General Washington ordered redoubts nine and ten to be taken the night of October 14. The Americans would charge redoubt nine and the French would seize number ten. But the redoubts were defended by abatises. These rows of sharpened branches could slice a man to pieces. The Sapper and Miner Corps would have to advance first, in silence. Armed with only knives and axes, they would clear a path.

Darkness fell. Joseph and the rest of his corps crawled beyond their trench. His eyes remained fixed on the sky, waiting for three shells to be fired from a nearby battery. That was the signal for the commanders to order their men to advance.

In 1781, Joseph Plumb Martin was only 20 years old. As he lay on his belly on the cold, damp ground, perhaps Joseph wished he had never taken up the mantle of a rebel. He could be safe and warm in front of his grandfather's fire. Was an independent nation worth death at the hand of a British bayonet?

Battle of Yorktown

Suddenly, three balls of fire rocketed into the sky. The code word for the miners and sappers to advance was *Rochambeau*. As this signal rippled down the line, Joseph thought it sounded like *rush-on-boys*.

And rush on he did. Joseph ran through the darkness, aiming for redoubt nine. Hand axes flew right and left. In minutes, the corps had cleared a passage through the abatises. Within 30 minutes, redoubt nine was in American hands.

At age 13, this young man believed he was a coward. But when confronted with the injustice of British rule and the hope of a future in a free and independent country, the boy became a rebel and helped his country win a revolution.

Soldier of the Revolution

Joseph Plumb Martin was mustered out of the army on June 11, 1783. He taught school for one year and then moved to Maine, where farmland was cheap and plentiful.

Joseph married and had five children, but he struggled to make a living. When the Revolutionary War ended, the only pay soldiers received for their years of service was their guns. Finally, in 1818, veterans of the American Revolution who could prove they were poor received a pension.

At age 59, Joseph testified in court that he was worth only $52. The government granted him a pension of $96 a year. In 1830, Joseph wrote a memoir of his experience as a soldier in the Revolutionary War. It was titled *Private Yankee Doodle: Being a Narrative of some of the Adventures, Dangers and Sufferings of a Revolutionary Soldier.* His rebellious spirit, still strong at age 70, is revealed in these words: "When the country had drained the last drop of service it could screw out of the poor soldiers, they were turned adrift like old worn-out horses. . . ."

Joseph Plumb Martin died on May 2, 1850. The epitaph on his tombstone reads: "A Soldier of the Revolution."

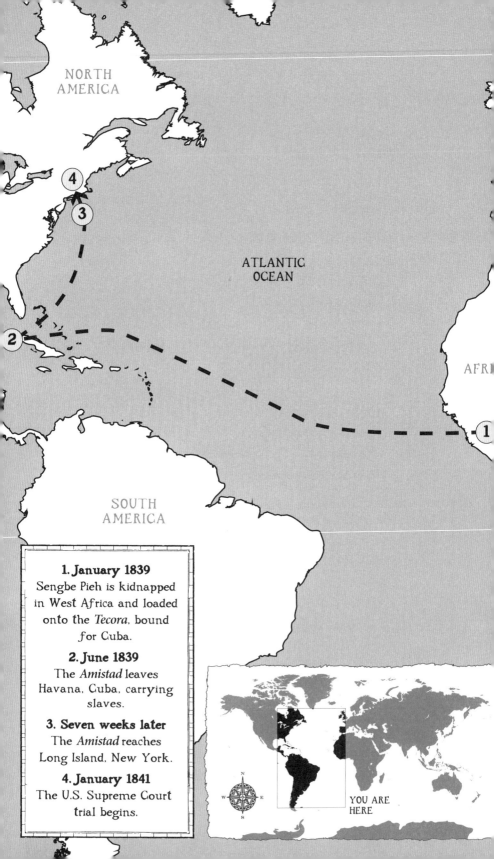

NORTH
AMERICA

ATLANTIC
OCEAN

AFRI

SOUTH
AMERICA

1. January 1839
Sengbe Pieh is kidnapped
in West Africa and loaded
onto the *Tecora*, bound
for Cuba.

2. June 1839
The *Amistad* leaves
Havana, Cuba, carrying
slaves.

3. Seven weeks later
The *Amistad* reaches
Long Island, New York.

4. January 1841
The U.S. Supreme Court
trial begins.

YOU ARE
HERE

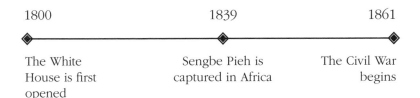

1800	1839	1861

The White
House is first
opened

Sengbe Pieh is
captured in Africa

The Civil War
begins

Chapter Two

Make Us Free

The 53 Africans—49 men, three girls, and
one boy—looked like an unlikely group of
rebels. The young and weak lay listlessly
on the deck of the ship, desperate for shade
from the harsh glare of the Caribbean sun.
The stronger men were chained below deck
beside casks of beef and bolts of cloth.

Most of the Africans were thin and all were filthy. Some lay in their own waste as death hovered patiently just behind them. Bloody stripes decorated the backs of others, courtesy of the ship's temperamental captain and the two Cubans who had purchased the African slaves a few days earlier. These men did not fear a ragtag group of slaves.

They should have.

In the dark hours before dawn on July 1, 1839, these scarred and beaten captives would launch a rebellion that shook the world.

In the 1460s, Portuguese explorers looking for a trade route to India landed on the West African coast. There, they found native people eager to trade. The Portuguese exchanged liquor, mirrors, velvet, brass, and muskets for ivory, furs, and slaves. Other European nations followed the Portuguese, and so the international slave trade was born.

After almost 400 years, this international trade in human flesh was banned. Slavery still remained legal *within* many countries, but slaves could not be traded *between* countries. However, the demand for slaves remained high.

Don Pedro Blanco was a Spanish slave trader who had come to West Africa in the late 1700s. He built a slave factory called Limboko at the mouth of the Gallinas River. A slave factory was where kidnappers brought their victims to wait to be sold to slave traders.

This area of Africa was home to many different tribes. Blanco hired some of the Kru people to work as his slave catchers. Blanco's business thrived and he became rich.

In 1817, the slave trade was banned, but Don Pedro Blanco continued his human trafficking operation. He sent Kru slave catchers a few hundred miles into the interior of the countryside to kidnap people he could sell into slavery.

Blanco was still in business on the morning in January 1839, when Sengbe Pieh said goodbye to his wife and three children. As this 26-year-old from the Mende tribe strode toward the rice fields, four strangers approached him. Before he could run, the men cast a net over him.

For the next few weeks, Sengbe was dragged around like an animal as the slave catchers rounded up more victims.

Eventually, the kidnappers turned west and marched the captives toward Limboko. Canoes ferried the hostages upriver, past forests of mangrove and cottonwood trees. The din of crickets and frogs almost drowned out the sorrowful cries of the people on the boats.

At Limboko everyone was stripped "perfectly naked" and Dom Pedro Blanco inspected the captives from head to toe. He rotated their arms and legs, examined their hips, armpits, and groins, pulled back their eyelids, and inspected inside their mouths.

Blanco ordered any diseased or mutilated people fed to the sharks in the bay.

The captives who passed scrutiny were housed in a barracoon. This bamboo corral with a thatched roof would hold the prisoners until a slave ship arrived.

For two months, Sengbe was locked in a barracoon with hundreds of other people. The living conditions were miserable. What the captives didn't know was how much worse things would get.

In April 1839, the slave schooner *Tecora* sailed up the mouth of the Gallinas River. Don Pedro Blanco stationed men in the cottonwood trees as lookouts for the British navy while the captives were loaded into canoes. The water was rough and boats often tipped, spilling captives into the shark-infested waters.

Sengbe climbed aboard the *Tecora* and the crew shoved him down the hatchway into the hold below. The Mende described death as "crossing the waters." The next eight weeks would have felt like death to Sengbe as he endured the crossing over the Atlantic, a trip called the Middle Passage.

The *Tecora* held between 500 and 600 captives. Sengbe and his countrymen spent 16 hours a day in a slave hold that sat four feet below the main deck. To create space for more slaves, a platform was inserted between the slave hold and the main deck. This meant the captives had only 22 inches of headroom.

People were packed in so tightly, they had to sleep pressed together like spoons in a drawer.

The male prisoners were shackled by the ankles, wrists, and necks. They were chained together in pairs, day and night. When the men needed to go to the bathroom, the Africans had to use what were called "necessary tubs," which were just large, open buckets placed in the hold. But often, they could not reach these tubs in time—remember, they were shackled together in a tiny space.

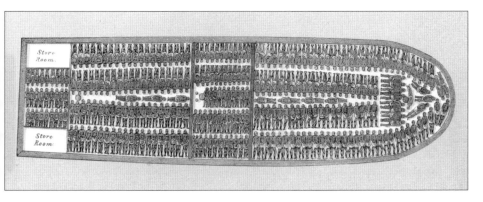

The layout of a slave ship

People were forced to lie in their own waste, blood, and vomit. Disease spread quickly. Each morning, the captives who had died the night before were hauled up on deck and dumped into the sea.

Sengbe tried to keep everyone's spirits up. He told them to get rid of their "sad faces" and asked them, "Is not ours a bold warlike nation?" He reminded the captives that they had been freemen once and would be freemen again.

One dark night in the middle of June, the *Tecora* slunk into the harbor of Havana, Cuba. Quietly, so as not to alert British naval patrols on the lookout for illegal slave traders, the Africans were loaded into rowboats and ferried to land.

For 10 days, the Africans stood alongside cattle, oxen, and sheep. The captives endured the poking and prodding of prospective buyers during slave auctions. Eventually, two Cuban men, Don Jose Ruiz and Pedro Montes, purchased Sengbe and 52 others, including four children.

On the moonless night of June 28, 1839, Ruiz and Montes disguised the captives in sailors' clothes and led them back to the waterfront. The two men were avoiding international authorities trying to crack down on illegal slave smugglers. A long schooner rode low in the water. Across its green and black stern was the ship's name—*La Amistad*.

Ruiz and Montes intended to sail along the Cuban coast to Puerto Principe, where Ruiz's uncle owned a plantation. *Amistad's* hold was packed with soap, glass knobs, guns, and barrels of fruit, olives, and beef. Half the Africans were kept on deck, and the rest, the strongest men, were chained in the airless hold.

Only a few casks of water had been taken on board for what was expected to be just a three-day voyage.

Sengbe might have hoped the crew of this new ship would be kinder than the crew of the *Tecora*. But Captain Ramón Ferrer hit the slaves with any hard object he could lay his hands on and Celestino the cook delighted in tormenting them.

The Africans were fed meager rations twice a day, but they suffered from thirst more than hunger. Captain Ferrer allotted them only half a cup of water twice daily.

While the Africans sat under the brutal sun with parched throats, the crew washed their clothes in fresh water.

Celestino taunted an African named Kinna by standing in front of him and guzzling down water. When Kinna and some others discovered a water cask in the hold, they drank from it. They were caught and the captain whipped their backs. Adding to the cruelty, he rubbed a mixture of salt, rum, and gun powder into their wounds.

On June 30, Celestino's taunting went too far. He drew his butcher knife across his throat and then made a chopping motion with the knife and put his hand to his mouth. Celestino gestured to a barrel of salted beef. The Africans were convinced they would soon be slaughtered and eaten.

Celestino probably assumed he was terrifying the Africans. He was, in fact, galvanizing them into action.

That night was dark and cloudy. A storm blew up and it began to rain. The sailors furled the sails. Eventually, the rain stopped and the crew fell asleep on the damp deck.

In the hold below, no one was sleeping. Sengbe had found a loose nail on the *Amistad's* deck and hidden it in his clothing. The men debated their next step.

"That man makes my heart burn," said Grabeau, speaking of Celestino, the cook.

"No one ever conquered the Mende," said Lubos.

"Who is for war?" asked another man.

The verdict was one word: "WAR!"

Two of the men in the hold were skilled blacksmiths. Sengbe handed them the nail. In the airless, reeking hold, everyone watched the blacksmiths painstakingly pick the main padlock that held everyone's chains to their neck collars. One by one, their shackles fell off.

The rebellion began before dawn, at 4 a.m. Sengbe slowly lifted the door of the hatchway. He climbed out first, followed by Faquorna, Moru, and Kimbo. The men crept past the other sleeping Africans. Glancing around the deck, Sengbe picked up a belaying pin and handspike. His countrymen did likewise.

They snuck toward Celestino, who lay sleeping in the ship's longboat stored near the cabin. The four men raised their makeshift weapons over their heads and clubbed the cook to death. The only sound was the meaty thud of wood on flesh and bone.

It was enough to wake Captain Ferrer. "Attack them," he cried. "They have killed the cook!"

The crew reached for their weapons as the Africans lunged at them. The captain fought fiercely with a dagger and a club. The two sailors did not have time to load their muskets and fought with their bare hands. Montes sprang from his cabin, a knife in one hand and a pump handle in the other.

The remainder of the captives poured out of the hatchway armed with machetes they had found in a crate. Sengbe ordered them to attack the captain, who fell under their blows and did not rise again.

Realizing they were hopelessly outnumbered, the two sailors threw a canoe overboard and leaped into the sea. They rowed furiously toward Cuba, 18 miles away.

The Africans seized Montes and Ruiz. Rage consumed Sengbe, and he wanted to kill them both, but Burna held him back. The Africans needed the Cubans, and agreed to let them live. Ruiz and Montes were locked in the slave hold.

The masters had become the captives.

When the sun rose, the Cubans were hauled back up on deck. Antonio, the cabin boy, had learned a few words and could communicate with the Africans. With Antonio translating, Sengbe ordered Montes to "steer toward the rising sun."

The Africans were going home.

By day Montes followed orders, but at night he reversed direction. The Cubans were desperate for another vessel to come close, even a British naval patrol. But whenever another ship approached, the Cubans were locked below deck. The crews on the other ships stared warily at the vessel full of black men armed with machetes and sailed on.

Water quickly became a problem. There were not enough containers on the ship to store water. When they were close to land, Sengbe ordered Montes to stop at a deserted stretch of beach so a search party could find a creek and refill their few barrels. This worked in the short term, but after six weeks, they were almost out of water and out of sight of land. Montes was convinced they were all going to die.

"Should we steer for the United States?" he asked Ruiz. The Cubans knew it was their only hope.

"Would you like to go to a free country where there are no slaves?" Montes asked the Africans.

They did not trust him, but Sengbe knew they had no choice. Eight men had already died from dysentery and dehydration. Montes steered west.

On their seventh week at sea, *La Amistad* reached Long Island off New York. The men anchored the ship and a small group went to shore to find water. They found a stream and, as the men were loading water into the rowboat to take back to the ship, two white men came down to the beach. Captain Henry Green and Captain Pelatiah Fordham had been hunting when they spotted the Africans.

Through hand gestures and Antonio's broken translation, Burna questioned the men. "What country is this?"

Green replied, "America."

"Is this slavery country?"

"No, it is a free country."

At the news that they had reached a free land, the Africans danced and whooped with joy. Green and Fordham were terrified and ran to their wagons to retrieve their guns. Burna tried to calm the white men down by explaining that they just wanted to go home. He gestured to the *Amistad*. "Make sail and go," he ordered, hoping the white men knew how to sail.

But Green and Fordham had other ideas. By now, everyone had heard reports of the mysterious "black schooner" that had been zig-zagging along the coast. Rumors claimed it was full of gold. These two men wanted it.

But while Green and Fordham were trying to convince the Africans to let them board the *Amistad*, a ship appeared on the horizon. The United States naval brig, the *USS Washington*, was commanded by Lieutenant Thomas Gedney. When he saw the *Amistad* at anchor and a group of men on shore, he assumed it was a smuggling operation. When Sengbe spotted the *Washington* headed for the *Amistad*, he ordered everyone into the boat and they rowed furiously for the ship.

But Gedney reached it first. He sent an armed party on board. The American sailors forced the Africans below deck and freed Ruiz and Montes. Sengbe saw the *Amistad* had been captured and he turned the rowboat around and headed back to shore. But a boat of American sailors caught them quickly and towed them to the *Amistad*.

Sengbe could not bear the thought of being chained in the slave hold again. As he was boarding the ship, he dove into the sea. What followed was a 40-minute game of cat and mouse. The Americans pursued Sengbe in a boat, but whenever they drew close, he dove deep under the water. Five minutes later, he would pop up elsewhere and the Americans would chase him down again. Finally, the sailors slipped a boat hook under his clothes and hauled an exhausted Sengbe out of the water. He was put in chains.

The Africans were back where they had started—in the hold of slave ship.

———◆———

Spectators gathered by the hundreds along the wharf at New London, Connecticut. The *USS Washington* was towing what appeared to be a ghost ship. Torn sails hung loose from the masts. Barnacles and sea grass fouled the hull.

Federal Marshal Norris Wilcox took possession of the captives and started the legal process rolling. On August 29, Judge Andrew Judson boarded the *Amistad* to hold a hearing. He would determine if there was enough evidence to charge the Africans with piracy and murder.

Judson ordered Sengbe brought on deck. The African man listened intently while the judge questioned Ruiz and Montes. He understood nothing but was convinced the Cubans were lying.

Ruiz and Montes did lie. They presented false papers to show the Africans had been born as slaves on Cuba. Then the judge questioned the cabin boy, who said Sengbe, Muru, and Kimbo had murdered the cook. That was enough for Judson. He ordered the Africans held in jail in New Haven, Connecticut, until their trial on September 17.

Witnessing the hearing that day was an abolitionist named Dwight Janes. Janes studied the Africans and then sidled over to Ruiz.

"Can they speak English?" he asked the Cuban.

"A few words."

"Can they speak Spanish?"

"Oh no." Ruiz shook his head. "They are just from Africa."

The Cuban had just admitted that he had broken international law.

Perhaps he assumed since Janes was a white man, he would not object. But as soon as Janes returned to shore, he notified other abolitionists.

Opponents to slavery had always existed in American history, but they were not organized or strong. In 1833, this changed when the American Anti-Slavery Society was formed. The movement was small, but vocal. The Anti-Slavery Society published newspapers and sent pamphlets into the Southern slave states. It petitioned Congress to change the laws. Abolitionists came from all walks of life—whites and free blacks, men and women, rich and poor.

Like the *Amistad* Africans, the abolitionists were rebels. Instead of machetes, they used the power of words to persuade their fellow Americans that slavery must be abolished. Abolitionists would be the Africans' greatest allies in their fight for freedom.

◆

The physical strength of Sengbe and the other men could not help them escape the iron bars of their New Haven jail. The Africans needed to tell their story.

On September 10, 1839, the wealthy New York merchant and abolitionist Lewis Tappan arrived at the home of Marshal Norris Wilcox. Tappan was accompanied by the linguist Josiah Gibbs, an attorney named Roger Baldwin, and James Ferry, a former slave from West Africa. Ferry spoke Vai, a language one of the Africans named Bau could also speak.

The marshal brought Sengbe and Bau into the room. As though they were playing a strange game of telephone, Tappan asked a question in English, Ferry translated it into Vai, and Bau translated it into Mende so Sengbe could answer. Bit by bit, the captives' story was revealed.

On September 14, 1839, Marshal Wilcox arrived at the jail to transfer the Africans to Hartford, Connecticut, for their trial. Crowds thronged the streets of Hartford. Judges, lawyers, journalists, abolitionists, and curiosity seekers descended upon the courthouse.

More than 4,000 people filed into the jail to peer through the bars at the Africans. Sengbe stared back. What was he thinking? What was he feeling?

When their hearing began on September 19, the Africans had no clue that their fight for freedom would play out against the backdrop of greed and power. It seemed everyone wanted the Africans.

Amistad prisoners

Lieutenant Gedney, the commander of the *USS Washington,* claimed the ship and captives belonged to him because he had "salvaged" them. This was a kind of "finders-keepers" law of the nineteenth century. Henry Green and Pelatiah Fordham, the two men the Africans had met on the Long Island beach, argued they deserved salvage rights.

Montes and Ruiz claimed they had purchased the slaves and were their rightful owners. A representative of the Spanish government spoke on behalf of the dead Captain Ferrer, insisting his estate be compensated for the ship, the dead cook, and Antonio the cabin boy. Finally, a lawyer speaking for the administration of U.S. President Martin Van Buren argued the slaves and ship should be returned to Spain, since Cuba was a Spanish colony.

The judges who heard the case quickly dismissed the charges of murder and piracy. But the question of who owned the Africans was not resolved. A third hearing was scheduled in January 1840.

Spectators who came for drama found it.

Through their interpreter, Sengbe, Grabeau, and Fuli testified. Sengbe sat on the floor to show the judges how he had been chained. Grabeau and Fuli lay down side by side to demonstrate the cramped quarters of the slave hold. All three men described the terror they felt when Celestino the cook mimed how he planned to chop and eat them.

Finally, the judges concluded that the captives were "natives of Africa and were born free and . . . still . . . are free and not slaves." They ordered the federal government to return the Africans to their homeland.

When the interpreter translated the verdict, Sengbe and the others were overjoyed. They clapped their hands and jumped up and down.

During their months in captivity, the Africans had been learning about Christianity, along with beginning lessons in reading and writing. Now, an abolitionist minister began to pray. The Africans joined him, dropping to their knees in thanks.

Their relief was short lived. The Van Buren administration immediately appealed the decision to the United States Supreme Court.

The news of this reversal crushed the Africans. Sengbe lost weight. Other men were convinced they would never see their families again. Foone, an accomplished swimmer, dove into the river one day and drowned himself. But as weeks turned into months, the Africans slowly regained their spirit of resistance and concentrated on winning in court.

Geography books, dictionaries, and almanacs were brought to the jailhouse. The Africans read and talked and debated. When they learned that former president John Quincy Adams would argue for them in the Supreme Court, they recruited their two best English writers, Kale, who was only 11 years old, and Kinna, to write letters to Adams.

The arguments in these letters represented the united effort of all the captives—they referred to themselves repeatedly as the Mende people.

In the letter penned by Kale, the Africans urged President Adams to challenge the public belief that they were stupid savages. "Americans no talk Mende. Americans crazy dolt?!" Kale wrote.

He went on to explain that the insults in the American newspapers hurt their feelings. "Some people say, 'Mende people have no souls,'" Kale wrote. "Why we feel bad, we have no souls?" The Africans were making a logical argument.

The letter Kinna wrote appealed to Adam's emotions. "We want to go home to Mende and see our fathers and mothers and brothers and sisters."

He communicated the prayer that Adams had the "heart to see Mende people." With these words, the Africans were asking this powerful white man to recognize the humanity he shared with them. The letter closed with a plea.

"We beg you to talk hard. You make us free . . ."

Adams did "talk hard." On February 24, 1841, nine U.S. Supreme Court justices assembled to hear the arguments in the case of the *United States v. the Amistad*. All the justices were white and most of them were Southern slave owners.

John Quincy Adams defended the Africans in a marathon, seven-and-a-half-hour argument. He twisted the government's legal position—how could the Africans be property and robbers of property?

While Adams paced back and forth, he frequently referred to the principles of the Declaration of Independence and pointed at the copy of that document that hung on the wall. He laid out logical arguments, cited evidence, and used moral reasoning to persuade the justices that "these negroes were free and had a right to assert their liberty."

On March 9, 1840, in a seven-to-one ruling, the Supreme Court said that while the murders of the captain and cook had been "dreadful acts," they were not criminal. The Africans had been acting in self-defense. The justices sided with the decision of the lower court when they ruled that "these negroes never were the lawful slaves of Ruiz or Montes or of [anyone else]." After an almost three-year struggle, the Africans had finally won their freedom.

"What will you do now?" an abolitionist asked. "Return to Africa or stay in America?"

Fuli answered for everyone. He insisted that even if the America people gave him a hat full of gold and houses and land to stay in this country, these things were "not like his father, nor his mother, nor his sister, nor his brother." The *Amistad* Africans were going home.

To raise funds for a ship and supplies, the former captives went on a sort of celebrity tour during the spring and summer of 1841. They spoke at gatherings throughout New England, telling their story, performing songs, and demonstrating their knowledge of English. The grand finale of each show was Sengbe. Speaking in Mende, he acted out the story of the *Amistad* rebellion. Although the audience could not understand a word he said, everyone was spellbound by his performance.

Finally, on November 26, 1841, the Africans boarded the *Gentleman* for a reverse Middle Passage. Five missionaries accompanied them. The Christian abolitionists and former captives planned to work together to spread the word of God in Sierra Leone.

The *Gentleman* docked in the city of Freetown on January 13, 1842. The Africans tumbled onto the shore, hugging their countrymen. More than two-thirds of the Africans deserted the mission and headed into the countryside to locate their lost families. Sengbe returned home only to find that his village had been destroyed and his wife and children stolen by slave catchers. He eventually returned to the mission, where he worked as an interpreter until his death in 1879.

CANADA

WASHINGTON

MONTANA

OREGON

IDAHO

WYOMING

②

NEVADA

UTAH

CALIFORNIA

COLORADO

①

ARIZONA

NEW MEXICO

MEXICO

1. 1923
Sierra Madre, California
Yosh Kuromiya is born.

2. Fall 1942
Wyoming
Yosh and his family are
forced from their home
to Heart Mountain
Relocation Camp.
In Spring 1944, Yosh
refuses to report to the
U.S. Army.

YOU
ARE
HERE

1939   1942   1945

WWII begins   Japanese internment   WWII ends
in Europe   camps are established

Chapter Three

The Heart Mountain Resisters

The letter arrived in the morning mail on March 16, 1944. Yosh Kuromiya had been expecting this, and dread filled his stomach as he opened the envelope.

Order to Report for Pre-Induction Physical Examination

It was as Yosh had feared. He was being summoned.

The world had been embroiled in the bloodbath of World War II since 1939. The United States was fighting Germany in Europe and Japan in the Pacific. Yosh was a healthy 21-year-old. He would certainly pass his physical, be inducted into the army, and sent to Europe to fight.

Rebels and Revolutions

Outside the dingy window of Yosh's quarters, row after row of army barracks squatted on the barren Wyoming plain. This garrison was surrounded by a barbed-wire fence and guard towers. Beyond the fence loomed the snow-covered foothills of Heart Mountain.

A chill settled on Yosh's heart. He had a terrible choice to make: obey the law and defend his country or break the law and defend his principles.

Yosh was a Nisei. This term refers to a person of Japanese ancestry living in the United States. Yosh's parents had been born in Japan. They joined the wave of Japanese people who emigrated to the west coast of the United States in the late nineteenth and early twentieth centuries. Yosh's parents settled in southern California.

These first-generation Japanese immigrants, or Issei, faced much discrimination. Because they spoke a different language, were Buddhist, and looked different from whites, the newcomers were labeled the "Yellow Peril." Laws were passed to prevent the Issei from becoming full members of American society.

They were barred from becoming American citizens, forbidden to buy land, and not allowed to eat in certain restaurants. In 1924, the federal government cut off all further immigration from Japan.

But Yosh Kuromiya was a Nisei, the child of Japanese immigrants. He had been born in the United States and was a citizen. The Nisei were as American as their white neighbors.

The Nisei spoke English, joined the Scouts, studied the U.S. Constitution in school, listened to swing music, and played baseball.

However, like their parents, the Nisei faced racial discrimination. One afternoon, Yosh was hanging out with some buddies at the house of a white friend. The boys had been climbing trees in the backyard and decided to go in the house. Just as Yosh was about to enter, someone slammed the door shut and locked it.

Thinking it was a joke, he waited. And waited. No one opened the door. Yosh realized what this meant.

He was the only Japanese boy in the group and he was not wanted.

Nisei children were taught to ignore such insults. If a Nisei girl was not invited to a classmate's birthday party, her mother would say, "It can't be helped." If a teacher told a Nisei boy that he was forbidden from serving on the student council because of his race, the boy's father would advise him to "Just endure it." If a group of Nisei youth got in trouble for walking through a white neighborhood, their parents would insist they never make that mistake again because, "The nail that sticks up, gets hammered."

Most Issei raised their children with sayings that reflected Japanese principles. Avoid conflict and keep a low profile. That was considered the best way to assimilate into America.

The Nisei who took these lessons to heart formed the Japanese American Citizens League (JACL) in 1930. The JACL leaders were older, educated Nisei—the doctors, lawyers, and college professors. They worked to gain acceptance in the United States.

The lower-class, less-educated Nisei such as Yosh thought the JACL was a stuck-up social club run by rich people who did not understand the concerns of poor Nisei. By 1940, the United States government considered JACL to be the voice of all Japanese Americans.

Soon that voice would be saying something Yosh did not want to hear.

Sunday, December 7, 1941, dawned over the city of Honolulu on the island of Hawaii. The sun shone over the row of American battleships anchored in the Pearl Harbor naval base. A cluster of clouds clung to the mountain peaks in the center of the island, but the rest of the sky was sapphire blue. Waves slapped against the shore and seagulls squawked. The landscape was tranquil and beautiful.

At 7:55 a.m. this peaceful world exploded.

Out of nowhere, Japanese planes filled the sky, diving low over the battleship row and the nearby airfields. Sirens began to blare and American sailors raced on deck, some still in their pajamas. As the men looked to the heavens, bombs began to fall.

More than 350 Japanese aircraft blasted Pearl Harbor for almost two hours. Eight battleships were destroyed or damaged, and 11 other ships sunk. Almost 200 American airplanes were destroyed.

The greatest tragedy of the day was human. A total of 2,335 American service people were killed and more than 1,000 wounded. There were also more than 100 civilian casualties.

With one swift blow, Japan pushed the United States into joining World War II.

The *USS Shaw* exploding in Pearl Harbor

The day after the attack on Pearl Harbor, U.S. President Franklin D. Roosevelt declared war on Japan. A few days later, Germany and Italy, Japan's allies, declared war on the United States. America now had to fight a war on two fronts—Europe in the east and Japan in the west.

The morning of the attack on Pearl Harbor, 19-year-old Yosh Kuromiya was working at his parents' produce stand in southern California. When his white customers told Yosh not to worry because "everything would be all right," he was irked. "Those [attackers] were Japanese from Japan," he recalled later. "I'm an American." It bothered Yosh that people linked him to the enemy.

That was just the beginning. In the days following Pearl Harbor, government agents swept through Japanese communities along the West Coast, arresting more than 1,300 Issei. Government propaganda posters and political cartoons depicted Japanese people as ape-like, sly, and barbaric.

Anyone with Japanese features was called "Nip," "Jap," or "yellow."

As the Japanese military scored one victory after another in the Pacific, Americans on the West Coast panicked. They began to eye the Nisei with suspicion.

The director of the FBI concluded that the Nisei did not represent any security threat, but racism can be stronger than reason. Politicians and journalists fanned the flames of public hysteria. People feared the Nisei might spy for Japan or commit sabotage.

Lieutenant General John DeWitt, the head of the military command in the western states, believed all Nisei on the West Coast should be deported. In early 1942, he said "the Japanese race is an enemy race." Although the Nisei were American citizens, Dewitt believed their "racial strains" were "undiluted."

Newspaper columnists agreed. One wrote "Herd em up, pack em off . . . . Let em be pinched, hurt, hungry, and dead up against it." The Nisei were Americans, but they looked like the enemy. Therefore, they were treated like the enemy.

As the public outcry grew louder, the government cast a noose around the Nisei and slowly tightened it. President Roosevelt acted first. In February 1942, he signed Executive Order 9066. This rule authorized the U.S. War Department to identify military zones from which anyone could be excluded.

A curfew came next. On March 24, 1942, General DeWitt ordered all Nisei living on the West Coast to be confined to their homes from 8 p.m. to 6 a.m. As the sun stayed up later each day that spring, Yosh stood by his window and watched white neighbors go for an evening stroll or out with friends. He could not join them.

The curfew was only the beginning. At the end of March 1942, General DeWitt announced that the War Relocation Authority would deport all Nikkei from California, Oregon, and Washington. They were ordered to prepare for relocation to a "temporary residence elsewhere."

Yosh wondered how long *temporary* would be and where *elsewhere* was.

The JACL cooperated with War Relocation Authority officials to help the deportation go smoothly. No one talked of resisting the deportation. The JACL wanted to prove the Nisei were loyal Americans. Going along peacefully with the deportation would demonstrate their patriotism.

Yosh Kuromiya's family had two weeks to put their affairs in order before they had to report to a temporary assembly center at the racetrack in Pomona, California. Yosh was an art student enrolled in a community college. He had to drop out.

Ordered to bring only what they could carry, the Nisei raced to sell their houses and sell or store their cars, furniture, and other belongings. Farmers, such as Yosh's parents, were forced to leave their crops in the ground to rot.

Many Nisei families did not own vehicles, so they rode school buses to their assigned assembly center. But Yosh's family had a pickup truck. Hoping to find a way around the luggage rule, they loaded the truck with their most valuable possessions and drove to the Pomona racetrack.

The guard at the gate ordered the Kuromiyas to take only what they could carry from the back of the truck and leave the rest. For the next few days, Yosh could see their truck parked just beyond the fence. One day it disappeared. He never saw the truck or their belongings again.

When the Nisei entered the assembly center, they were each handed an empty cloth bag and ordered to fill it with straw. These bags served as their mattresses. Yosh's family was housed in a long barracks that had been divided into 20-by-20-foot rooms. Each family lived in one room, bare except for a single light bulb and army cots.

Gaps between the tops of the walls and ceiling meant there was no privacy, but the Kuromiyas had it better than the deportees who were housed in old horse stables. The walls and floor of those rooms were saturated with horse urine and covered in horse hair.

More than 5,000 people had to share just 36 showers and toilets.

Yosh endured a long, hot summer at the Pomona assembly center. Meanwhile, the War Relocation Authority hastily built 10 camps to house 110,000 Nisei for the long term. These concentration camps were located in California, Utah, Wyoming, Arizona, Colorado, and Arkansas. By the fall, the residents of Pomona were on the move again.

Heart Mountain Relocation Center,
Heart Mountain, Wyoming

As the train chugged through pine forests and up snow-topped mountains, Yosh could almost pretend he was going to summer camp. The Heart Mountain Relocation Camp was in Wyoming, a state he had never visited. So far, the scenery was beautiful and images of canoe races and marshmallow roasts ran through his mind.

Then, the train descended to a desert as dry and barren as the moon. When Yosh saw the Heart Mountain Relocation Camp sprawled out before him, the fantasy evaporated. With barbed-wire fencing, guard towers, search lights, and military police, this was no summer camp. This was a prison.

Yosh stepped off the train and into a dust storm. Gusts of wind stirred up sand into a blizzard that shot dirt up his nose and into his mouth and ears. He later described Heart Mountain Camp as "a godawful place."

Rows of army barracks stood as if waiting inspection. Each barrack was 20 feet wide by 100 feet long and divided into five rooms.

Yosh shared a 20-by-20-foot room with his parents and two sisters. The walls and floorboards were warped, allowing the wind and snow and bugs to creep in. Empty orange crates became shelving and stools. Each group of 12 barracks shared communal bathroom and shower facilities, as well as a recreation room and mess hall, where a lot of barely edible rice was served.

The Nisei tried to create a version of their old lives. The children attended classes. People planted gardens. The camp started its own newspaper, the *Heart Mountain Sentinel*. But as the months dragged on and the war showed no sign of ending, Yosh wondered if he would be imprisoned forever.

In fact, the JACL was working to get some of the Nisei out of the camps.

Mike Masaoka, the leader of the JACL, wanted the army to draft them. If Japanese-American blood was spilled in defense of the country, no one could claim the Nisei were not loyal citizens. The problem was that, after Pearl Harbor, the military had classified all Nisei as 4C—"aliens not accepted to the armed forces."

Masaoka fought this prohibition. Masaoka told the delegates gathered for a JACL conference, "Somewhere on the field of battle, in a baptism of blood, we . . . must prove to all that we are ready and willing to die for the one country we . . . pledge allegiance to."

The JACL voted to petition the government to draft the Nisei. When the delegates returned to their camps, they were nervous. They had to tell these men behind barbed wire that they might get their freedom soon— if they were willing to die for it.

President Roosevelt liked the idea of Japanese Americans fighting for their country. That winter, on February 1, 1943, he announced the formation of the 442nd Regiment, an all-Nisei combat team.

The government called for volunteers, hoping for at least 3,600. But there was one catch. The War Department refused to allow any Nisei into the army until their loyalty was checked.

On February 6, 1943, registration teams were sent into the camps to sift the loyal Nisei from the disloyal. But instead of questioning just draft-age men, the officials used a questionnaire to interrogate every adult in camp—male and female, Issei and Nisei. It was a disaster.

Two questions proved to be the stumbling block.

Question 27: Are you willing to serve in the armed forces of the United States on combat duty whenever ordered?

This was a trick question. If the Nisei answered no, would the government think they were disloyal? But if they answered yes, could they immediately be sent into combat?

Question 28: Will you swear . . . allegiance to the United States of America and faithfully defend the United States . . . and foreswear any allegiance . . . to the Japanese emperor . . . ?

Question 28 stunned the Issei. They were forbidden by law from ever becoming American citizens. Now the United States was asking them to give up their Japanese citizenship.

They would be a people without a country.

This question was a slap in the face to the Nisei. They were American citizens who had never been loyal to the Japanese emperor. Why should they have to foreswear an allegiance they never had?

The registration was a failure. Fewer than 6 percent of fighting-age Nisei volunteered to join the 442nd Regiment. Worse, by the end of 1943, more than 9,000 people had asked the government to send them to Japan. Most of these requests were from Nisei.

Meanwhile, newspapers railed about the "disloyal Japs." Congress held an investigation and decided to isolate the "disloyal" Nisei. In the fall of 1943, some 19,000 Nisei were transferred to Tule Lake, a camp for troublemakers in California.

Back at Heart Mountain, loyal Nisei who had no desire to move to Japan felt angry and betrayed by the loyalty questionnaire. They had suffered through deportation, imprisonment, and interrogation simply because of their race. These Nisei had done their best to follow their parents' advice and *just endure it.*

In 1944, the government took another step, one that proved unendurable for many Heart Mountain men.

On January 20, 1944, the government announced the Nisei would be drafted. By early February, men at Heart Mountain began receiving notices telling them when a bus would arrive to take them to the city of Cheyenne for their pre-induction physicals. If they passed the medical exam, they were going to war.

Yosh was worried and bitter. He might be sent to risk his life in war while his family remained locked up. That was not a principle he was willing to die for.

A few weeks before the draft was announced, a man named Kiyoshi Okamoto had organized a group called the Fair Play Committee (FPC). This group held meetings in one of the mess halls to talk about how it could improve life in the camp. When word of the draft reached them in January 1944, the FPC members began to debate this issue.

The evening of February 8, 1944, the FPC held its first public meeting. About 60 men showed up to hear Kiyoshi Okamoto speak. He was not a lawyer, but Okamoto knew a lot about the Constitution and the Bill of Rights. He laid out a logical argument about why drafting men who had been denied their civil rights was against American values.

Yosh attended the meeting. He was skeptical, so he sat in the back of the room in case he decided to sneak out. But Yosh wound up staying for the entire meeting, and returned the next night, too.

Okamoto put to words the feelings that had been churning in Yosh ever since he heard about the draft. What the government was asking of him was unjust. Yosh became a member of the FPC.

There were three requirements for members: You had to be a Nisei, you had to be absolutely loyal to the United States, and you had to be willing to serve in the military *once your civil rights had been restored.* The FPC wanted to be clear. They were not traitors. They were loyal resisters.

Interfering with the draft was a crime punishable by five years in jail and a $10,000 fine.

The *Heart Mountain Sentinel* was the camp's newspaper, controlled by members of the JACL. The paper printed articles that cast the leaders of the Fair Play Committee as "clever troublemakers" and "deluded youth." The editor of the *Heart Mountain Sentinel* called on the FBI to arrest them.

The FPC leaders stepped up their resistance. On March 4, 1944, they circulated a letter throughout camp calling on Nisei to disobey the draft. In the letter, FPC leaders agreed that the Constitution must be defended because it guaranteed the "freedom, liberty, justice, and protection of all people." But, they continued, "have we been given such freedom, such liberty, such justice, and such protection? NO!"

In the letter, they insisted that if Nisei did not resist such "injustices and discriminations IMMEDIATELY, the future of all minorities and the future of this democratic nation is in danger." They urged members not to report for their pre-draft physicals.

FPC members listened. On March 6, two men refused to board the bus for Cheyenne to take their physicals. The next day, three more men refused. And so it went. Day by day, the resistance grew.

Yosh Kuromiya was ordered to report for his physical on March 23. He considered swallowing a bottle of soy sauce before the exam. He had heard soy sauce caused the blood pressure to skyrocket. But Yosh decided that was the coward's way out. The time had come for him to submit or fight.

At the next meeting of the Fair Play Committee, one of the leaders asked who had a physical scheduled soon. Yosh raised his hand.

"What will you do?" the leader asked.

Yosh felt a million eyes on him. The pressure was intense. If he went to war, the nation and most of the Nisei community would hail him as a hero. If he refused, he would be prosecuted as a traitor and could go to jail. Ultimately, Yosh's conscience overrode his fear.

"I will not be on that bus," he said.

The room erupted in cheers, and Yosh slumped back on the bench. He knew he had "passed the point of no return."

Late in the afternoon of March 25, several large black cars pulled up in front of the Heart Mountain barracks. Families wept as federal marshals led away sons, brothers, and husbands. The community was stunned, but the resistance did not dampen. A few days later, 25 more men refused to report for their physicals.

The government had had enough. The two top leaders of the Fair Play Committee, Sam Horino and Kiyoshi Okamoto, were transferred to the segregation camp at Tule Lake. Another seven FPC leaders were jailed and charged with conspiracy to counsel young men to evade the draft.

By June 1944, 63 draft resisters, including Yosh Kuromiya, were behind bars in the Cheyenne jail awaiting trial on draft evasion.

June 6, 1944, was D Day. The American military landed an invasion force of 150,000 men on the northern coast of France to push the German army east. World War II was not over, but it was the beginning of the end.

Not so for the Heart Mountain resisters. One week after D Day, they went on trial. Yosh was relieved when the trial date finally arrived, because conditions in the Cheyenne jail were unbearable. Built to house only 30 people, all 63 draft resisters were crammed inside. Mattresses lined the cell floors and were squeezed into the corridors.

Twice a day, guards shoved food between the cell bars. However, the meals were so awful that the men flushed most of the food down the toilet. The inmates had no visitors because their families remained locked up at Heart Mountain. They were not allowed to go outside, and spent 24 hours a day caged up.

On June 12, 1944, the trial of the "Heart Mountain 63" began. It was the largest mass trial in Wyoming history. On the advice of their lawyer, the men had waived their right to a jury trial. Their fate was solely in the hands of Judge T. Blake Kennedy. He had a reputation as hardworking and was well-respected by other members of the legal community.

Yosh and the other resisters felt optimistic about their chances for acquittal.

That hope evaporated on the first day of the trial, when Kennedy referred to the defendants as "you Jap boys." The trial ended on June 20, 1944. All 63 men were found guilty of violating the draft and sentenced to three years in prison.

Other trials followed that of the Heart Mountain 63. Although draft resistance was less organized at the other concentration camps, there were men at eight camps who refused to report for their physicals.

Ultimately, 315 Nisei, including the seven leaders of the Fair Play Committee, were imprisoned for draft violations. Their sentences ranged from two to five years in federal prison.

Only one judge defied the pattern of conviction. In the Northern District of California, Judge Louis Goodman presided over the trial of 27 men. Goodman said the government's decision to draft people it had unjustly locked up was "shocking to the conscience." He dismissed the charges against all 27 men. The government did not appeal this verdict.

The convicted Nisei were held in federal prisons in Kansas, Washington, and Arizona. In August 1945, while the resisters were still behind bars, the United States dropped atomic bombs on two Japanese cities, one on Hiroshima and a second on Nagasaki. Japan surrendered and World War II ended.

Two days before Christmas of 1945, U.S. President Harry Truman pardoned all the Japanese American draft resisters. Finally, they were free to take their place as full citizens again.

In a 1993 interview, Yosh Kuromiya was asked why he resisted the draft. He said he had no choice.

"As an American citizen . . . we all had an obligation to raise the issue of the incarceration [and] evacuation . . . ." When Yosh refused to submit to the draft, he did not know how severely he would be punished, but he was willing to take the risk. In Yosh's words, "Somebody had to say something."

In 2000, the Japanese American Memorial to Patriotism During World War II was erected at the National Mall in Washington, DC. The memorial depicts cranes entangled in barbed wire, and the names of the Nisei soldiers who died in World War II are carved on the walls surrounding the monument. The words President Truman spoke to the Nisei soldiers when they returned from Europe are on display: "You fought not only the enemy, but you fought prejudice—and you won. Keep up that fight . . . to make this great republic stand for just what the Constitution says . . . the welfare of all of the people all of the time."

Missing from this monument are the names of the Heart Mountain resisters and the rebels at the other camps who followed their consciences.

KENTUCKY

TENNESSEE

NORTH CAROLIN

SOUTH CAROLIN

MISSISSIPPI

ALABAMA

Montgomery

GEORGIA

FLORIDA

GULF OF MEXICO

☮ March 2, 1955,
Montgomery,
Alabama

Claudette Colvin refuses to
give up her seat on a bus
and becomes part of the
Civil Rights Movement.

YOU ARE
HERE

N
W E
S

1865   1950s   1956

◆━━━━━━━━━━━━━━━━━━━━━━━━◆━━━━━━━━━◆

Slavery officially ends   The Civil Rights   The Alabama
in the United States   Movement begins   bus boycott
                                                    ends

Chapter Four

A Cry for Justice

Jim Crow lurked everywhere in Montgomery,
Alabama, in the 1950s. You could see racism
by drinking fountains and restrooms, in
movie theaters and schools, at restaurants
and clothing stores. A teenager named
Claudette Colvin grew up with Jim Crow,
and she played by its rules year after year.

One day, Claudette decided she'd had enough of Jim
Crow. Her cry for justice launched a movement that
transformed not just the American South, but the
entire country.

When Claudette was born in 1939 in Birmingham,
Alabama, Jim Crow had ruled the state for decades.
Jim Crow was not a person, but a way of life.

"Jump Jim Crow" was a popular song after the Civil War that made fun of African American culture. The phrase "Jim Crow" became the label for the system of laws and social customs that treated African Americans as second-class citizens. Jim Crow laws kept African Americans segregated from whites.

From birth to death, a line divided white and black people—this line was dangerous to cross.

Black babies could not be born in white hospitals. Black children could not attend white schools. Blacks could not use white waiting rooms, restrooms, swimming pools, or parks.

Jim Crow laws created a Jim Crow mindset. A white person called a black man "boy," not "sir" or "mister." A black person never shook a white person's hand because it implied equality. In a vehicle, blacks were always made to sit behind whites, never beside or in front of them.

Claudette did not notice Jim Crow much in the first years of her life because she lived in the tiny, all-black community of Pine Level, about 30 miles from the state capital of Montgomery. Claudette was raised by her great-aunt and great-uncle, Mary Ann and Q.P. Colvin. She considered them her parents and called them Mom and Daddy Q.P.

Claudette ran free through the neighborhood with her best friend, Annie. They climbed trees and wandered trails and meandered in and out of the homes of her parents' many friends.

School and church were the center of Claudette's life. She loved learning and was so good at it that she skipped second grade. Claudette never missed church, especially "Big Meeting Sunday." This one Sunday a month, Reverend H.H. Johnson came to preach, and the sermons, singing, eating, and games lasted from noon until dusk. In Pine Level, Jim Crow kept its distance, and Claudette grew up feeling self-confident and secure.

When she turned eight, everything changed. The family moved to the big city of Montgomery, Alabama. The Colvins' new house was in a working class neighborhood known as King Hill. Narrow houses lined unpaved streets and an outhouse stood in each backyard. Daddy Q.P. did yard work for a white man, and Mom was a maid for a white family.

Jim Crow stalked Claudette throughout the city. When she went dress shopping, Jim Crow did not allow African Americans to try on clothes in the dressing room. If Claudette needed new shoes, Mom traced her bare feet on a brown paper bag and took the pattern to the store for the clerk to match.

Jim Crow said no black feet could test shoes a white person might later buy.

Oak Park, the nicest park in Montgomery, was only a few blocks from Claudette's house. But Jim Crow ordered black folks never to play ball or rest on a bench there.

But where Jim Crow irritated Claudette the most was on the city bus. Each bus had 36 seats. The first four rows were reserved for whites only. All riders, black and white, boarded the bus at the front door and deposited their fare in the coin box. Then, if any white person was on the bus, blacks had to get off and reenter the bus by the rear door.

Drivers constantly checked their rearview mirror. If the white seats were full, a driver would order blacks to give up their seats to a white person. No African American could sit level to or ahead of a white rider.

So if four African Americans were sitting in a row and one white person needed a seat, all four blacks had to stand.

Few African Americans owned cars, so they had to endure the daily humiliation of the buses to get to work and school. The Montgomery Bus Lines hired tough men, and city law gave them police-like powers. Some even carried guns.

Bus drivers often referred to African American passengers as "black cows" and "black apes." It was dangerous to resist.

In 1952, a black man named Brooks was shot to death by police after he walked down the aisle past white people instead of using the rear door. The police officer was not charged because authorities said Brooks was resisting arrest, so it was a "justifiable homicide."

In the fall of 1952, tragedy struck just as Claudette entered Booker T. Washington High School. Her little sister, Delphin, had contracted polio that summer and she died in September, on Claudette's fourteenth birthday.

A few weeks later, Jeremiah Reeves, a friend from Claudette's neighborhood, was arrested for raping a white woman. After a short trial by an all-white jury, Reeves was convicted and sentenced to die.

The black community was convinced Reeves was innocent. The National Association for the Advancement of Colored People (NAACP) was a national civil rights group with a local chapter in Montgomery. When members of the NAACP began to work on an appeal for Reeves, Claudette joined the cause. She attended rallies, wrote letters to Reeves in prison, and raised funds for his defense.

"Jeremiah Reeves's arrest was the turning point of my life," Claudette later said.

The U.S. Supreme Court threw out Reeves's conviction and ordered Alabama to retry him.

Claudette Colvin

Unfortunately, the boy's second run at justice was no better than the first. The jury took only 34 minutes to sentence him to death again.

Anger filled Claudette. She was sick of being pushed around by white people, but she did not know what to do to change things. Then, two high school teachers helped Claudette channel her anger into action.

Geraldine Nesbitt and Josie Lawrence were teachers at Booker T. Washington High School. Nesbitt taught English literature and Lawrence taught history. These women did not follow the white school board's assigned lessons. Nesbitt taught the required writing of Edgar Allan Poe and Nathaniel Hawthorne, but her students also read the Magna Carta and U.S. Constitution. Reading these documents, Claudette began to mentally understand what she had always felt emotionally.

Jim Crow was illegally depriving her of her rights as an American citizen.

In history class, Josie Lawrence celebrated African heritage. She taught students that their culture did not begin on slave ships, but instead had a long and rich history on the African continent. Josie Lawrence was a very dark-skinned woman who proudly proclaimed that she was "a pure-blooded African."

The most popular girls in school were the ones with the lightest skin. Kids with dark skin, such as Claudette, were often called "nappy-headed." Most girls spent hours with hot combs trying to straighten their kinky hair. They were trying to look white.

By this time, change was in the air in schools across the South. In 1954, the U.S. Supreme Court had issued a landmark decision in *Brown v. the Board of Education of Topeka, Kansas*. The court ruled that segregated schools were unconstitutional and they must integrate with "all deliberate speed."

In some communities, integration went smoothly, but in other places, it was violent.

Claudette had only one year left of high school and would finish it out at all-black Booker T. Washington. After that, she vowed to go to college and study law. Then, she planned to return to Montgomery and work to defeat Jim Crow.

In February 1955, Booker T. Washington High School celebrated Negro History Week. Nesbitt and Lawrence turned it into Negro History Month.

Claudette soaked up lessons about African history and culture and about black heroes and celebrities. Every day, she left school fired up to take a stand.

She was tired of worrying about whether her skin was too dark or her hair too curly. She was tired of listening to adults complain about inequality but not act to change things. "I was tired of hoping for justice," Claudette remembered. "When my moment came, I was ready."

Her moment came on March 2, 1955.

That muggy spring afternoon, Claudette walked to the bus stop with her friends after school. The yellow and green city bus pulled up, and Claudette climbed on board. She dropped her fare in the coin box and, because there were no whites on the bus, Claudette and her friends proceeded down the aisle.

Claudette chose a window seat in the middle of the bus. One of her friends sat beside her and two other classmates sat in the row directly across the aisle. Claudette stacked her textbooks neatly in her lap and stared out the window.

The bus stopped at every corner and more people got on. The rows reserved for whites filled up quickly. Suddenly, Claudette glanced up. A white woman was standing in the aisle, waiting for Claudette and the other three students to give up their seats.

The bus driver looked in the rearview mirror. "I need those seats."

Claudette studied the white woman. She was not old or sick or pregnant. She did not deserve a seat more than Claudette. They had paid the same fare.

But Jim Crow was not about fairness. It was about white superiority.

Claudette's friends stood up and went to the back of the bus. The white woman now had three empty seats to choose from. But she would not sit down because Claudette, a black girl, would be sitting beside her, not behind her.

All the brave black women Claudette had studied in history class that month ran through her mind. They had stood up for justice. Now, it was her turn.

Years later, Claudette said, "I could not move because history had me glued to the seat. It felt like Sojourner Truth's hands were pushing me down on one shoulder and Harriet Tubman's hands were pushing me down on another shoulder."

"Why are you still sittin' there?" the driver yelled.

Claudette did not move or reply.

The driver scowled in the rearview mirror. "Get up, gal!"

Claudette stared straight ahead. She could feel outrage radiating off the white woman standing in the aisle.

The bus driver drove a few more blocks and then pulled over behind a squad car. A tense silence fell over the bus. Claudette swallowed and tried to slow down her racing heart as she watched two policemen enter the bus.

"Who is it?" an officer asked. The driver pointed at Claudette.

Both officers walked down the aisle and loomed over her.

"Aren't you going to get up?" the officer asked.

"No, sir," she replied.

"Get up!" he shouted.

Claudette began to cry. "It's my constitutional right to sit here as much as that lady." Nerves made her voice high pitched. "I paid my fare. It's my constitutional right."

Each officer grabbed one of Claudette's arms and yanked her up. Her textbooks flew to the ground. Claudette knew better than to struggle so she went limp. One of the officers kicked her and they dragged her off the bus.

"It's my constitutional right," Claudette repeated as they shoved her into the back of the squad car. Through her tears, Claudette saw blurry black and white faces peering at her through the bus windows.

The ride to the police station was torture. The policemen taunted her. They made rude comments about her body. Claudette put her handcuffed hands together and prayed.

Although Claudette was only 15, she was taken to the city jail, where adult criminals were held. An officer led Claudette to a cell, pushed her in, and slammed the door. When the guard turned the key in the lock, Claudette said, "It was the worst sound I ever heard . . . . It said I was trapped."

She fell to her knees and "prayed like I'd never prayed before." Old Jim Crow had won this round.

Claudette's jail stay was short, but her upcoming battle would be long and grueling. Her mother and Reverend H.H. Johnson bailed Claudette out. On the ride home, the reverend told Claudette he was proud of her. "Everyone prays for freedom, but you're different . . . . I think you just brought the revolution to Montgomery."

The black community agreed. Claudette returned home to a jubilant welcome. Word of her brave stand spread throughout King Hill.

People gathered at the Colvin house. Everyone hugged and praised Claudette. Claudette was warmed by all the positive attention, but terrified of her upcoming trial.

Fred Gray was one of Montgomery's two African American attorneys. He had long wanted to mount a legal challenge to Jim Crow, and he agreed to represent Claudette. A group of black leaders met with the police commissioner and the manager of the bus company. Among these leaders was 26-year-old Martin Luther King Jr., the new pastor of the Dexter Avenue Baptist Church.

The meeting was cordial and the bus company admitted that Claudette had not been sitting in a "whites-only" seat. She technically had not broken the law. But the police commissioner refused to drop the charges. Claudette would go to trial.

Gray went to the Colvin house to make sure Claudette and her family knew the danger they faced. Claudette was tackling Jim Crow head on. The Ku Klux Klan, a white supremacist terrorist group, had lynched people for less.

"Are you sure you want to do this?" Gray asked.

"Yes, I am," Claudette answered.

On March 18, Claudette's case was heard in juvenile court in front of Judge Wiley Hill. Claudette faced three charges: breaking the segregation law; disturbing the peace; and assaulting the police officers.

The police officers testified that Claudette had kicked and hit them as they tried to peacefully remove her from the bus. They read a letter from a white passenger who described the policemen as gentle and said they spoke so quietly that other passengers could not even hear them.

Thirteen black students who had been on the bus also attended the hearing. Their testimony contradicted the police, as the students described how the officers yelled at Claudette and kicked her before dragging her off the bus. Fred Gray argued that Jim Crow violated the protections every citizen of the United States was given by the Constitution. But this defense was useless.

Judge Hill issued a quick and harsh verdict. Claudette was guilty on all charges. She was placed on probation, made a ward of the state, and released to the custody of Mom and Daddy Q.P.

The judge banged the gavel. Court dismissed.

Despair washed over Claudette and she began to weep. She was a convicted criminal just because she had not given up her seat to a white person.

Despite her disappointment in the verdict, Claudette was not ready to give up her fight for justice. She waited as the civil rights leaders struggled with what reaction they should take to the verdict.

One option was to boycott the city buses. Three-fourths of the riders were black. If African Americans stayed off the buses, the city's transportation system would go broke.

But the black community was worried. If they launched a boycott now, Claudette would be the face of the movement. She was only 15. Some of the adults questioned whether a rebellious teenager would follow their guidance.

Plus, the Colvins came from a different social class than the city's civil rights leaders. Her great-aunt and great-uncle, Mary Ann and Q.P., had dropped out of school after the sixth grade. They both performed manual labor for whites. The family lived in King Hill, a neighborhood with a rough reputation. Claudette was described as too "emotional" and "feisty."

The civil rights leaders decided to wait for a better role model to inspire a bus boycott. Leaders helped her raise money to appeal her case and then they left her alone.

On May 6, 1955, Fred Gray went to court to appeal Claudette's conviction. This time, a different judge heard the case and he dropped two charges. Now, she was guilty only of assaulting the police officers. But she still had a criminal record. Claudette's rebellion had gotten her nothing but trouble.

And Jim Crow was still alive and well on Montgomery's buses.

When she returned to school for the last few weeks of her junior year, Claudette was no longer the brave rebel. Attitudes had hardened against her. Students saw her as a troublemaker and mocked her with a sing-song chant: "It's my constitutional right. It's my constitutional right."

Claudette was isolated and lonely, but found a way to fight back. She gave up straightening her hair and braided it into cornrows. Everyone was stunned the day Claudette walked into school with a head full of braids. She was ridiculed, but she held her chin high and told everyone, "I won't straighten my hair until they [the government] straighten out this mess."

Summer vacation arrived. Since Claudette was afraid to go to dances or parties with other teenagers in case she might accidentally violate her probation, she spent hours alone.

Soon, Claudette found herself in an even bigger mess.

Church and NAACP youth group meetings were her two social outlets. The youth group meetings were led by Rosa Parks, a middle-aged seamstress and civil rights activist.

Claudette liked Parks, who was an intelligent, kind woman, but she felt uncomfortable with the other kids at the meetings. They were the children of educated professionals who attended private high schools. Gradually, Claudette stopped going to youth group meetings. She felt more isolated than ever.

One day, Claudette met someone who made her feel less lonely. She was watching a ballgame at King Hill Park when a man struck up a conversation with her. He was in his mid-20s and married, but was separated from his wife. The man told Claudette to ignore the people who teased her for wearing braids. He complimented her on standing up for what she believed in.

Claudette knew she was in dangerous territory hanging out with a much older, married man, but he made her feel good about herself again. She kept on seeing him. When summer ended and her senior year began, Claudette was pregnant. Shortly before Christmas, the principal called her to his office.

Claudette had expected this.

"I know why I'm here," she told him. "You don't need to say it."

The principal said it anyway. A semester short of graduation and Claudette's education was over. She'd been expelled.

Everyone turned their backs on her—friends, teachers, and civil rights activists. Then, just as Claudette went into exile, the spark she had lit on a bus one afternoon finally burst into flame. But all Claudette could do was watch from the sidelines.

———◆———

On December 2, 1955, Rosa Parks refused a bus driver's command to give up her seat for a white person. That weekend, activists distributed tens of thousands of leaflets in factories and stores, in restaurants and beauty parlors, in church pews and on street corners. The leaflet told of the arrest of Rosa Parks and urged "every Negro to stay off the buses Monday in protest of the arrest and trial . . . ."

In the light-skinned, soft-spoken, respectable Rosa Parks, the civil rights leaders had found the face to launch the movement that Claudette had begun.

The black community responded, and on Monday, December 5, the buses ran empty. That evening, a mass rally was held at a black church. Nearly 1,000 people wedged into the pews and thousands more gathered on the street outside.

Dr. Martin Luther King Jr.

Dr. Martin Luther King Jr. spoke. Just that day, he had been elected leader of a new civil rights group, the Montgomery Improvement Association (MIA).

This was King's first public speech outside of his sermons. He promised that blacks in Montgomery would fight until "justice runs down like water and righteousness like a mighty stream." A vote was held on whether to continue the boycott until Jim Crow was kicked off Montgomery's buses.

The verdict was unanimous—stay off the buses until black people could sit where they wanted.

When Claudette heard that Rosa Parks had been arrested and a boycott was launched, she was glad an adult had finally taken a stand. But she had done exactly the same thing that Parks did, almost a year earlier. Although Claudette had great respect for Rosa Parks, being forgotten and excluded "really, really hurt."

The city of Montgomery dug in its heels and the boycott continued. Blacks who owned cars donated them for use in community car pools. More than 40 pickup stations sprang up around the city, where volunteers drove people to and from work. Thousands of people walked. By late January of 1956, the bus company was losing $3,200 a day.

The police cracked down on protestors. They arrested Martin Luther King Jr. for driving five miles over the speed limit and he spent a night in jail. Two officers threw acid on another civil rights leader's car as it sat parked beside her house and then fled in their squad car.

———◆———

As the boycott continued, Claudette wanted to be part of the movement. "I'd had justice on my mind for a long time." Being pregnant did not change her passion for equality.

Church rallies were held two nights a week to keep people's spirits up. Embarrassed by her pregnancy, Claudette attended rallies at churches outside her neighborhood so she did not run into people she knew. Although she could not play much of a role, she wanted to help keep the boycott going.

One morning Fred Gray knocked on the Colvins' front door. Claudette had not heard a word from him since her appeal. Gray was there on serious business. Since the U.S. Supreme Court had ruled that segregated schools were unconstitutional, then segregated buses must be, too.

The NAACP was mounting a legal challenge in federal court. Instead of fighting for one rider at a time, the organization was filing a class action suit on behalf of all black bus riders. Gray needed plaintiffs. These people would testify in court about the harm Jim Crow buses had caused them. Gray needed brave people who could stand up to the white power structure. Gray had four other women, but he really wanted Claudette to join the lawsuit.

As Claudette listened, two thoughts struck her. The Ku Klux Klan would resist this lawsuit with every weapon of terror at its disposal. Her blood ran cold as she imagined men in white hoods coming to King Hill at night. But another thought ran on the heels of this image: She did not want to live in fear.

"Yes, I'll join the suit," she told Fred Gray.

Claudette gave birth to a baby boy on March 29, 1956. While she learned how to be a new mother, she also prepared for her day in court.

On May 11, 1956, Claudette rose early and dressed with care. Daddy Q.P. accompanied Claudette to the courthouse. A crowd of people, mostly African Americans, was gathered on the sidewalk. The men wore suits and the women dressed in their Sunday best. Reporters and cameramen milled about. The courthouse doors opened and everyone filed inside.

Claudette and the other plaintiffs sat beside their legal team on the right side of the chamber—the city attorney and defense witnesses were seated on the left. The three-judge panel sat in high-backed chairs at the front of the chamber, flanked by flags of the United States and Alabama. Spectators filled the main floor and balcony.

One by one, the plaintiffs testified to how they had been mistreated on Montgomery's buses. The strategy of the city's attorney was to cast the boycotters as puppets of Dr. King who had not minded the segregated buses until he came along and stirred things up. Claudette was scheduled to testify last. A knot tightened in her stomach as she waited for her turn.

"Call your next witness," the judge ordered.

"I call Claudette Colvin," Gray said.

Claudette stood ramrod straight as she swore to tell the truth. A sea of black faces lay before her. In the back of the courtroom, one of her neighbors gave her a thumbs up. Gray took Claudette step by step through the events of March 2, 1955.

Then it was the city attorney's turn. Time and again, he tried to trick Claudette into painting Dr. King as the mastermind of the bus boycott.

"Did you have a leader?" the attorney demanded.

"Our leaders is just we, ourselves," she replied.

Claudette carefully dodged the attorney's tricky questions. She knew Dr. King had not put her up to anything. She had challenged the Jim Crow bus system because she was sick of being treated like a second-class citizen.

"Why did you [Negros] stop riding the buses on December fifth?" the attorney asked.

"Because we were treated wrong, dirty and nasty." Claudette's gaze was steady and her voice strong.

The city attorney gave up. "No further questions."

It took the judges only 10 minutes to reach a decision, but they waited more than a month, until June 19, to announce it. In *Browder v. Gayle*, the court ruled for the plaintiffs. The court found the Montgomery bus system unconstitutional.

City officials immediately appealed the decision to the U.S. Supreme Court, so the bus boycott continued. Finally, on November 13, 1956, the news was announced. The Supreme Court had affirmed the lower court's decision. On December 20, two federal marshals served Montgomery with orders to immediately integrate the buses.

After 381 days, Montgomery's bus boycott was over.

The next morning, Dr. King and several other activists boarded a bus, dropped their fare in the coin box, and took seats in the front rows. Claudette Colvin was not among them. A single mother struggling to make ends meet, Claudette watched the nation embrace Rosa Parks as the hero who launched the Montgomery bus boycott. The girl whose bravery started the revolution faded into the shadows, just a footnote in history.

Claudette eventually earned her GED, equivalent to a high school diploma. She had another child, became a nurses' aide, and settled in New York City. She assumed her role in desegregating Montgomery's buses had been long ago forgotten. She was wrong.

On the 50th anniversary of the bus boycott, Claudette was invited to speak to the student body of Booker T. Washington High School. The experienced thrilled her. It was five decades late, but she was finally receiving recognition as a fighter for justice. When the students asked Claudette what advice she had for them, she said, "Don't give up. Keep struggling."

Claudette came to understand that Rosa Parks was the right person to represent the Civil Rights Movement at its birth. But Claudette also knew that she had carried an important message too. "Mine was the first cry for justice," she recalled, "and a loud one."

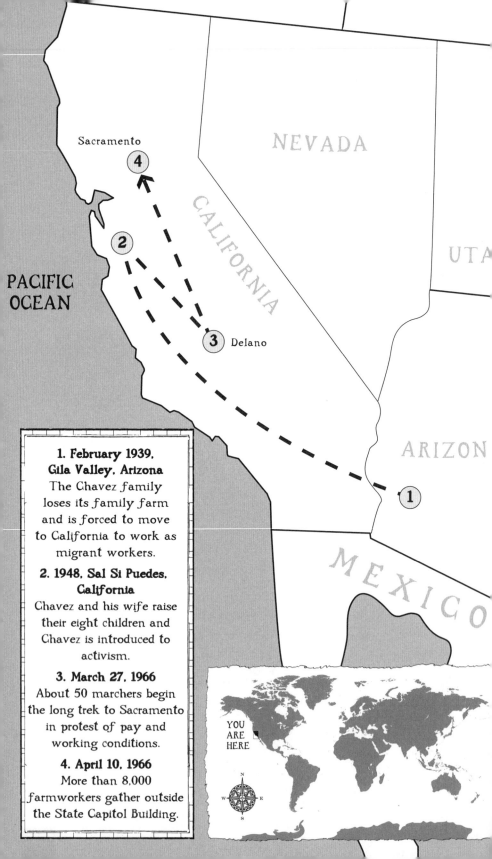

Sacramento

④

②

PACIFIC
OCEAN

NEVADA

CALIFORNIA

UTA

③ Delano

ARIZON

①

MEXICO

**1. February 1939,
Gila Valley, Arizona**
The Chavez family
loses its family farm
and is forced to move
to California to work as
migrant workers.

**2. 1948, Sal Si Puedes,
California**
Chavez and his wife raise
their eight children and
Chavez is introduced to
activism.

3. March 27, 1966
About 50 marchers begin
the long trek to Sacramento
in protest of pay and
working conditions.

4. April 10, 1966
More than 8,000
farmworkers gather outside
the State Capitol Building.

YOU
ARE
HERE

N
W—E
S

1938	1963	1970

| The Fair Labor Standards Act is passed | President John F. Kennedy is assassinated | The farmworkers' contract with grape growers is signed |

Chapter Five

Viva La Causa

Twelve-year-old Cesar Chavez stood rooted to the soil of what had been, until a few days ago, his family farm. It was February 1939, the height of the Great Depression. Cesar's parents had been unable to pay the taxes on their land in the Gila Valley of Arizona, so the state sold their ranch to the highest bidder.

Cesar's father loaded their belongings into the family station wagon and Cesar's mother wept. The day his family lost their land was the day rebellion was born in the heart of Cesar Chavez.

His grandfather fled poverty in Mexico in the 1880s and homesteaded 100 acres in Arizona just over the California border. Cesar's father, Librado Chavez, also farmed the land, growing cotton, watermelon, and alfalfa. He opened a grocery store and pool hall in the valley.

Although Cesar's childhood home did not have indoor plumbing or electricity, the family made ends meet. Then, the stock market crashed in 1929, and the nation plummeted into a decade-long depression. In 1933, a drought struck. Soon, the Chavez family could not pay its bills. The family joined hordes of other landless farmers heading to California to work in the agricultural industry.

California agriculture began in the 1860s. White men purchased large tracts of land to grow fruit, nuts, and vegetables. They needed labor to work these fields and turned to the cheapest source available— immigrants. First the Chinese, then Filipino and Japanese workers toiled in the fields. In the early 1900s, 1 million Mexicans joined them.

When the Chavez family arrived in California, they had to compete for work with 300,000 other desperate farm laborers.

As migrant workers, the Chavez family traveled up and down California to follow the seasons of the crops. They would spend two weeks on one farm harvesting watermelon and then two months on another farm picking grapes. Some migrant workers rented rooms, some slept in tents, and many lived in huge camps run by labor contractors.

There was money to be made in the California fields, but these profits did not trickle down to migrant workers such as Cesar and his family. The white landowners, called growers, paid labor contractors a fee to hire migrant workers for planting or harvesting.

The contractors charged the workers rent to live in the labor camps. The growers paid the migrant workers an hourly wage and a set amount based on how many rows a worker planted or harvested. But the growers could change the wages they paid whenever they wanted, and they often did.

---◆---

In a barrio of San Jose called Sal Si Puedes, Cesar and 10 other people slept in a 10-by-12-foot room. A broken-down garage with a dirt floor served as the kitchen. Cesar's mother, Juana, cooked over an old bathtub that she filled with firewood and covered with a grill.

The Chavezes struggled to put food on the table.

Wherever they moved for work, the Chavez children went to school and worked in the fields on weekends and holidays. Cesar and his younger brother, Richard, also worked odd jobs. They ran errands for people, shelled walnuts, and collected foil from cigarette wrappers to sell to the junk man. The boys turned over every cent to their mother.

Cesar's skin color and Mexican heritage made him a target. One day, Cesar went into a cafe and ordered a hamburger. The waitressed laughed and said, "We don't sell to Mexicans."

The movie theater in the city of Delano was segregated. In 1944, Cesar sat in the whites-only section. The police were called and Cesar was hauled to the station and lectured.

Juana Chavez had never learned to read and write and insisted all five of her children attend school. But Cesar hated it.

Cesar said later, "We were like monkeys in a cage." Whenever any of the Mexican American children spoke Spanish, teachers forced them to run laps or write, "I won't speak Spanish," on the board hundreds of time.

One teacher even hung a sign around Cesar's neck with the words, "I am a clown, I speak Spanish."

The cruelty of the students was even more painful. Cesar had one "good" shirt for school. He wore this same gray T-shirt every day and washed it each night. The other students ridiculed him for never changing his clothes, but Cesar never lashed out. Juana Chavez raised her children to be nonviolent. She was famous in the family for her *dichos*, or sayings. One of her favorites was, "It takes two to fight, and one can't do it alone." Cesar took this philosophy to heart.

During his eight years of formal education, Cesar attended 37 different schools. When he graduated from eighth grade in June 1942, Cesar dropped out. He was only 15 years old when he went into the fields to work full time.

The life of a migrant laborer was hard and humiliating. Supervisors insulted and intimidated workers. There was no drinking water or bathrooms in the fields, so people went behind bushes when they could find them. Pesticides were sprayed over the fields while the workers bent over the crops.

Sometimes, the pay was so low and working conditions so bad that workers went on strike. Librado Chavez joined a few labor unions when Cesar was a teenager. A union is an organization made up of workers in a particular field. The workers negotiate as one united voice, which gives them more power.

The most powerful weapon a union has is a strike. Whenever Librado heard the word "huelga" (strike), he and his kids walked off the fields.

But growers defeated every union that tried to win a contract to represent migrant workers. Growers brought in strikebreakers, called scabs. There were always workers who were willing to work for lower wages than the union was demanding.

Cesar was desperate to find a way out of this hardscrabble life, but found himself with many mouths to feed. In 1948, he married Helen Fabela and the couple eventually had eight children. Cesar believed the only way to escape the poverty of a migrant worker's life was to help his children get an education. Then he met some men who helped him envision another option.

Cesar and Helen settled in Sal Si Puedes, where Cesar found a job stacking lumber. One day, he met Father Donald McDonnell, a priest who conducted services in a little shack he was trying to turn into a church. Cesar helped out by painting benches and doing carpentry.

McDonnell talked to Cesar about economics. Farm laborers earned a few dollars a day. They lived in tents or shacks and fed their children a diet of beans, fried dough, dandelion greens, and potatoes. The growers lived in mansions and drove expensive cars. They fed their children steak and the fresh vegetables and fruit that migrant workers picked but could not afford to buy.

McDonnell gave Cesar books about Gandhi, the Indian activist whose nonviolent resistance pushed Great Britain to give India its independence. Cesar learned about the federal laws that protected all American workers, except farm laborers.

Father McDonnell opened Cesar's mind to the possibility of social change.

Viva La Causa

Home of Mexican field worker showing water supply
photo credit: Library of Congress

One evening in June 1952, a stranger knocked on Cesar's door. Fred Ross ran a group called the Community Service Organization (CSO), whose mission was to help Mexican Americans. The CSO registered Mexican Americans to vote, taught English classes, and filed discrimination claims for people who had been mistreated.

Ross had worked with people in Los Angeles and wanted to expand into San Jose, where many Mexican Americans lived. Would Cesar hold a meeting at his house the next night?

"How many people do you want?" Cesar asked.

"About four or five," Ross said.

"How about 20," Cesar said. Ross was delighted.

The next night, 20 people packed into Cesar and Helen's little house. Ross spoke about the struggles Cesar and his neighbors faced and how much power poor people could have if they united.

Cesar began crisscrossing California for the CSO. He organized English classes and citizenship classes, he translated for people, wrote their complaint letters, and helped them navigate legal troubles.

In 1958, the CSO hired Cesar as its national director. As he met with poor Mexican Americans in one community after another, Cesar heard a common complaint: "We want jobs!" Labor contractors and growers were violating the law by hiring braceros—Mexican farm workers—instead of American citizens to plant and harvest their crops.

This was illegal. Braceros could be hired only in areas where there was a shortage of American workers. That was not the case in California, but the growers preferred to hire braceros because they could pay them less.

Cesar decided to test the growers' hiring system to expose their law-breaking. In Oxnard, there was a large bracero labor camp. Cesar showed up at the crack of dawn one morning to apply for a job in the fields. The labor contractor told him to fill out his application at the Farm Placement Service, eight miles away. Cesar did and was given a work registration card, which he took back to the bracero camp.

"Sorry," the man at the camp said, "all the jobs have been filled today."

Cesar learned the camp sent their braceros to the fields at 4:30 a.m. By 6:00 all work for the day had been assigned.

So, he tried a different approach. The next day, Cesar arrived at the bracero camp at 5:00 a.m. with his registration card from the day before in hand.

"Sorry," the labor contractor said. "I can't accept this registration. It's dated for yesterday."

It was time to organize. Cesar started to take others with him to the Farm Placement office to apply for work.

At first, only two or three people accompanied him. But within a month, 100 to 200 migrant workers were applying for work every day. They formed a line outside the Farm Placement office with Cesar at the head. When he shouted, "March," they filed inside and marched past the secretaries to the employment office in the back room.

The application form was designed to frustrate and confuse. An applicant had to recount his employment history going back 20 years! But Cesar talked the migrant workers through the form.

Cesar also tried a more visible tactic. Migrant workers picketed the bracero camp every evening, shouting, "We want jobs." When the U.S. Secretary of Labor spoke to businessmen in Oxnard, 1,000 migrant workers stood outside the building with signs that read, "We want jobs!"

Cesar's tactics worked.

The federal government began to investigate the growers' use of the bracero program.

About 13 months after this battle began, growers agreed to hire migrant workers instead of braceros, and they boosted wages from 60 to 90 cents per hour. Cesar knew this victory would be short-lived. He had organized thousands of people for a common goal, but there was no permanent structure in place to safeguard these hard-earned gains once he left the area.

Cesar's prediction came true. Six months later, braceros filled the fields around Oxnard again. Migrant workers needed their own labor union.

Only with a labor union could their interests be represented by a permanent group with the power to negotiate wages and working conditions. Growers could not be allowed to change the rules whenever they felt like it.

Cesar tried to persuade the rest of the CSO to support his vision. At the CSO convention in 1962, delegates voted on whether the organization should work to create a migrant workers' union. The "no" votes won. Cesar was there with Fred Ross and another farm activist named Dolores Huerta. Ross and Huerta both wept, but Cesar had another strategy.

As the convention was ending, he stood. "I have an announcement to make." Cesar paused and then dropped the bombshell: "I resign."

The crowd was stunned. People begged him to reconsider, but Cesar refused. "I'm going to start my own union," he told Huerta.

She thought he was out of his mind. Cesar was only one man. He had no money. Building a migrant workers' union was a monumental task.

But Huerta could not get Cesar's dream out of her head. Migrant workers needed a union. Cesar had the passion and maybe that would help him succeed where other efforts had failed. Huerta quit the CSO, too, and became Cesar's partner.

———◆———

When Cesar quit the CSO, he and Helen had eight children, $1,200, and no jobs. But Helen shared her husband's dream. They moved back to Delano and got to work.

Helen went to work in the fields. She rose at 4 in the morning, prepared her children's breakfasts and lunches, and then worked for 10 hours for 85 cents an hour.

While Helen planted and picked, Cesar organized. He went door-to-door across California's agricultural sector, explaining how a union could help migrant workers. Dolores Huerta, Reverend Jim Drake, and Cesar's cousin Manuel helped him recruit union members. House by house, town by town, people joined the movement. A mere 20 people became 30 and then 75.

Cesar named the union the National Farm Workers Association (NFWA) and scheduled its first convention.

Delegates gathered on September 30, 1962, in an abandoned theater in Delano. Manuel had designed a union flag. It hung in the auditorium, a black eagle in the center of a white circle on a bright-red background.

They adopted a series of goals: enroll migrant workers across the state into the union; negotiate contracts with growers; lobby for a minimum wage. They also adopted the motto "Viva La Causa"—long live the cause.

The morning of September 8, 1965, Filipino grape workers in Delano went on strike. They were represented by their own union, the Agricultural Workers Organizing Committee, which had demanded a raise from $1.25 an hour to $1.40. The growers had refused.

Word of the strike spread among the Mexican American grape pickers. Workers streamed into Cesar's office all day, asking what they should do. Cesar scheduled a union meeting for September 16 so members would vote on whether or not to join the Filipinos in the strike.

On the evening of September 16, hundreds of farm workers crowded into a Delano church. Many were dirty and tired from a day in the vineyards.

Cesar rose to speak, reminding the audience that on September 16 in 1810, the Mexican Revolution had begun. He told the crowd that the workers would defeat the growers, just as the Mexicans overthrew the Spanish. It was time to vote.

Strike or no strike?

The farm workers' response shook the church walls. *Viva la huelga! Long live the strike! Viva la causa! Long live the cause! Viva Cesar Chavez!*

The people had spoken and their leader would support their decision, but he insisted members vote on one more issue: Would the strike remain nonviolent? Cesar still carried the *dichos* of his mother.

La Causa would not succeed if hatred and revenge became the union's weapons. Members agreed—no violence.

◆

At 4:30 the next morning, Filipino Americans and Mexican Americans joined forces for the first time. Strikers formed picket lines along the road outside the vineyards and carried signs that said, "Huelga." They stood on tops of cars and shouted through megaphones, trying to convince workers in the field to join them.

Chavez at a rally in 1972
photo credit: Joel Levine

Strikebreakers were bused in from as far away as Texas. Growers blasted music from car speakers to drown out the strikers' chants. Farm supervisors ran trucks past the picket lines to stir up clouds of dust. Growers unleashed dogs on strikers and sprayed pesticides in their direction. Some even shot bullets over the strikers' heads. In keeping with their pledge of nonviolence, union members did not retaliate.

The police sided with the growers. Every person on the picket line was photographed by a police officer. Cesar and other union leaders were followed by law enforcement every time they left home.

Rallies were held every night to keep strikers motivated. Cesar told the people, "If we can keep our great strike peaceful, non-violent, and strong, we cannot lose." Strikers cheered and sang and prayed. They felt the power of unity.

But two weeks passed, and then three. The grapes were being harvested and the growers showed no signs of relenting. Cesar wanted to gain more attention. When the county sheriff warned picketers that shouting "Huelga" was illegal because the noise interfered with business, Cesar got an idea. He gathered together a group of women and ministers who were willing to spend a few nights in jail.

On October 19, 44 union volunteers, including Helen Chavez, Cesar's wife, gathered outside a ranch in Delano and shouted, "Huelga" as loudly as they could. The protestors were arrested and charged with disturbing the peace and unlawful assembly.

When word of the arrest reached Cesar, he was just about to give a speech to 500 university students.

Cesar told them what had happened and asked if they would donate their lunch money to bail the strikers out. By the end of the day, the union had collected 6,700 one-dollar bills and the sheriff's department had received 100 telegrams and 300 phone calls of protest.

Although the strike was gaining attention, the growers still did not back down. People became desperate as their bills mounted up. Some strikers found jobs in other crops or returned to their former employers. Tensions grew as family and friends faced each other across an increasingly thin picket line.

The strike seemed doomed.

Cesar wrote to clergy and civil rights groups and student organizations. He pleaded with them to help the struggling migrant workers. If they could donate money, that was great, but what he really needed was volunteers to join the fight. He offered three meals a day and a floor to sleep on.

The appeal worked. College students, hippies, civil rights activists, ministers, and nuns all flocked to Delano. This melding of cultures, races, and social classes was proof that a revolution was in the air. Cesar put these volunteers to work implementing his new strategy—the boycott.

Fall had arrived. Grapes were gone from the fields, but were still in stores. The union needed to convince people to stop buying them. Schenley liquor company owned a small vineyard near Delano. The union sent word across the country—to help striking migrant workers in California, do not buy Schenley products.

Next, the boycott expanded to table grapes. Volunteers tailed trucks as they left the Delano vineyards, and picket lines were set up along the drivers' routes. These pickets caused delays and sometimes blocked the delivery of grapes completely.

Members of the longshoremen's union refused to cross the migrant workers' picket lines to load crates on ships. Fruit destined for Asia rotted on the docks. People in power began to pay attention.

Democrats in Congress wanted to amend the National Labor Relations Act. This law protected the right of workers to form labor unions, but excluded farm laborers from these protections. In March 1966, public hearings on the proposed changes were scheduled in California. Robert F. Kennedy, a young senator from New York, was invited to attend.

Robert Kennedy was the brother of U.S. President John F. Kennedy, who had been assassinated in 1963. Union officials told Kennedy that 30 strikers had just been arrested because scabs had threatened to hurt them. Before the hearing broke for lunch, Kennedy quizzed Kern County Sheriff Leroy Galyen.

"What did you arrest them for?" Kennedy asked.

The sheriff said, "[The scabs] said, 'If you don't get them [the strikers] out of here, we're going to cut their hearts out.'"

Kennedy frowned. "How can you go arrest somebody if they haven't violated the law?"

"They're ready to violate the law," the sheriff said.

The crowd roared with laughter, and Kennedy suggested that during the lunch break, the sheriff should read the U.S. Constitution.

This was a powerful, symbolic moment for the migrant workers' struggle. An influential senator was publicly ridiculing a local sheriff for his support of big growers. Someone in power was finally on the side of the workers.

Union organizers got word that the California Fair Trade Act had been passed by the California legislature. This law gave growers a guaranteed minimum price for their wine. But the men and women who picked the grapes to make that wine were not guaranteed a minimum wage.

Cesar decided the strikers would make a pilgrimage to the place of power. They would march from Delano to the state capital of Sacramento, 300 miles away, through 33 cities.

———◆———

The morning of March 17, 50 men set off from Delano, sleeping bags slung over their shoulders. Mile after mile, they marched through towns and cities and past fields of cotton and citrus. From a distance, a serpentine line of strikers stretched along the valley, red union flags silhouetted on a blue sky. People lined the road to cheer the men on and each evening, as they straggled into a new town, the marchers were greeted with dinner and a rally.

But in some communities, the marchers walked by homes with tables in the yards covered in fancy linens. Signs on the tables read, "We use Schenley products."

Some drivers flashed marchers the finger as they zoomed past.

At the end of the first day of marching, Cesar's feet were covered in blisters and his right ankle had swelled to the size of a melon. The next day, the swelling reached his thigh and he shook with fever. Forced to ride for a couple days, he resumed the march with a cane, but admitted, "Every step was a needle."

The men entered Stockton 18 days into the march. They were joined by 5,000 people. Mariachi bands played and spectators draped the marchers with flowers. That night, Schenley officials called union officials. They wanted to deal.

Rebels and Revolutions

The next day, Cesar signed an agreement with Schenley. They recognized the union and promised to begin negotiating wages within 60 days. On Easter Sunday, more than 8,000 farmworkers and their supporters gathered in the park in front of the capitol building in Sacramento. The farm workers may have won the battle, but the war was not over.

A few growers followed Schenley's example and signed contracts with the union, but most still refused. The union shifted the boycott to Digiorgio, the largest grower in California, and one known for using violence against strikers.

Digiorgio was a sneaky opponent. To get around the grape boycott, the company borrowed the labels of other growers. So, Cesar expanded the boycott. He appeared on daytime television to tell supporters to boycott *all* table grapes from California and any store where they were sold.

Volunteers fanned out across the country to implement this strategy. Priests knelt in produce aisles and prayed over grapes. Candlelight vigils were held outside the homes of supermarket executives whose stores sold California grapes. Boycotters stalled cars in the entrances of stores where California produce lined the shelves.

While the growers lost money, they still refused to give in.

Frustration among union members grew. People had been picketing in Delano for two years, and the grapes were still being picked and shipped.

When a striker was run over by a truck driven by an angry grower, people wanted revenge. Strikers set fire to some water pumps and a grower's shed. The mood was ugly. Cesar was determined to bring everything to a halt until the violence stopped.

His solution? A hunger strike.

One day in February of 1968, Cesar stopped eating. After fasting for four days, Cesar called a meeting to tell the strikers what he was doing and why.

"I'm going to fast until everyone in the strike either ignores me or makes up their minds to be nonviolent," he said.

Then he went to 40 Acres, a shed that had been converted to union headquarters. Cesar did not want to fast at home, where Helen and his children would see him suffer.

The union hall erupted after Cesar left as everyone bickered about who was to blame. But as days passed, the strikers began to unite. Cesar's actions had jolted people. Their dedication to the cause picked up. Their volunteering increased.

Talk of violence ended.

The first seven days were torture. Cesar dreamed about food. But by the eighth day, lightness filled him. He did not need sleep, nor was he hungry. He buzzed with energy and his concentration was sharp.

Then the pain began. Two weeks into the fast, Cesar's back and joints began to throb. The calcium was leaching out of his bones. People streamed into 40 Acres, pleading with Cesar to eat.

Finally, on March 11, 25 days after it began, Cesar broke his fast at a Mass with 4,000 supporters, including Senator Kennedy. The national media attended. Cesar was too weak to speak, but a friend read a message he had written.

"Our struggle is not easy. Those who oppose our cause are rich and powerful . . . . We are poor . . . . But we . . . have our own bodies and spirits and the justice of our cause as our weapons."

By 1969, the grape boycott stretched across the nation. Grape shipments to Boston, Philadelphia, Chicago, and Toronto were completely shut down. Grapes rotted in warehouses. The growers had lost at least $25 million and were finally ready to deal.

On June 29, 1970, five years after the strike began, 29 growers from Delano came to 40 Acres to sign contracts with the union. They agreed to pay workers $1.80 an hour and donate 10 cents an hour to the Robert Kennedy Health and Welfare Fund. All hiring would be done through the union rather than labor contractors. Workers would be protected from pesticide exposure. It was the most successful contract for farm workers in American history.

When Cesar was asked why the UFWO had succeeded when so many other unions had failed, he said, "we set an example that . . . we [were] not going to abandon the fight, that we were going to stay with the struggle if it took a lifetime. And we meant it."

The contract with the grape growers did not end Cesar's work. He led a strike against lettuce growers and, in the 1980s, when grape growers reneged on their commitments to protect workers from pesticide exposure, Cesar led an international boycott of California table grapes.

In later years, the union faced internal strife and competition from other unions. It failed to secure contracts from many growers. Despite these troubles, Cesar Chavez remains one of America's great rebels for social change. His vision of *La Causa* altered the lives of all migrant workers and became a model of social change.

Glossary

abolitionist: a person who wants to outlaw slavery.

acquittal: a judgment that finds a person not guilty of a crime.

activist: a person who works to bring about social or political change.

agricultural: based on farming.

ancestry: describes the people from your family or country who lived before you.

appeal: to make an urgent request.

artillery: a division of the army that handles large weapons. Also large guns used to shoot over a great distance.

assimilate: to absorb a person or group into a larger group.

auction: a public sale of property to the highest bidder.

ban: to prevent by law.

barracks: housing for soldiers.

barracoon: an enclosure used to hold slaves.

battery: in the military, a fortified area for heavy guns.

belaying pin: a wooden rod used on a ship to secure a rope.

Bill of Rights: the first 10 amendments to the United States Constitution, which guarantee basic personal liberties such as free speech and religion.

blockade: to seal off a place to prevent people or goods from entering or leaving.

boycott: to refuse to buy, use, or participate in something as a means of protest.

braceros: a Mexican laborer who is permitted into the United States for a limited time period in order to perform seasonal work.

brothers-in-arms: soldiers fighting together.

casualty: someone killed or injured in battle.

chasm: a deep crack or hole.

citizen: a person who owes allegiance to the government of a country and is entitled to protection from that country.

civil rights: the rights of citizens to have political and social equality and freedom.

colonial: relating to the years 1607 through 1776, when people from Europe settled in colonies in America—which eventually became the United States of America.

colonist: a settler living in a new land.

colony: a group of people who form a settlement in a distant land, but remain under the control of the government of their native country.

commandeer: to take possession of something.

community: a group of people who live in the same area.

Glossary

compensate: to give something, usually money, to someone who has suffered a loss or damage to property.

concentration camp: a place where large numbers of people, especially political prisoners or persecuted minorities, are imprisoned.

Congress: the branch of the United States government that makes the laws.

consequence: the result of an event or condition.

Constitution: a document that contains the basic laws and principles of the United States government.

Continental Army: the army formed by the Second Continental Congress that fought the Revolutionary War against Great Britain.

corps: a branch of the military assigned to a particular kind of work.

crops: plants grown for food and other uses.

Declaration of Independence: the formal statement that declared the 13 American colonies were independent of Great Britain.

democracy: a system of government in which the primary power is held by the people who rule through their elected representatives.

deport: to expel someone from a certain area.

deprivation: not having the things needed for a comfortable or healthy life.

discrimination: treating people unfairly because of certain characteristics, such as their gender, race, religion, or sexual orientation.

draft: requiring someone to serve in the military.

drought: a long period of time without rain.

dysentery: an infection of the intestines resulting in severe diarrhea.

emigrate: to leave one's own country in order to settle in another country.

enlist: to voluntarily join the military.

evacuate: to remove someone from a certain place.

execute: to put to death.

federal: national, covering the whole country.

Filipino: someone from the Philippines.

forage: to search widely for food or provisions.

fortify: to strengthen with walls and trenches.

freedom: the ability to choose and act without constraints.

galvanize: to shock or excite someone into taking action.

garrison: a military post where troops are stationed.

Glossary

GED: a test taken in order for a person to get the equivalent of a high school diploma.

goods: things for sale or to use.

Great Depression: a severe economic slump characterized by high unemployment that lasted throughout the 1930s.

haversack: a small, sturdy backpack carried by soldiers.

haycock: a cone-shaped mound of hay in a field.

heritage: the cultural traditions and history of a group of people.

hold: the deep interior of a ship.

homestead: to settle and farm land.

human trafficking: illegally transporting people from one country to another to force them to work without pay.

hysteria: uncontrolled emotions by a mass of people.

immigrate: to come permanently to live in a foreign country.

import: to bring in goods from another country for sale.

independence: being in control of your own country, government, or actions.

induct: to formally enroll someone in the military.

infantry: soldiers trained to fight on foot.

injustice: something that is very unfair or unequal.

integrate: to bring people of different races together.

internment camp: a place where people are confined or imprisoned.

interpreter: someone who translates from one language into another.

intolerable: unable to be endured.

Issei: first-generation Japanese immigrants to the United States.

Jim Crow: the practice of segregating people in the United States.

justice: fairness and equality.

labor contractor: someone who works with a landowner to hire seasonal farm laborers.

legislature: the lawmaking body of government.

liberty: being free from unfair restrictions by the government.

lynch: an illegal execution by a mob.

Magna Carta: a British document written in 1215 that guaranteed fundamental rights and liberties. Its principles were used by America's Founding Fathers when they drafted the Declaration of Independence and the United States Constitution.

mariachi: traditional Mexican folk music.

memoir: an account of someone's personal life experiences.

Middle Passage: the forced journey by enslaved people from West Africa to the Caribbean.

migrant worker: a farm laborer who moves from place to place to perform seasonal work.

migrate: to move from one place to another.

military: the army, navy, air force, and other armed services that protect a country and fight in wars.

militia: a group of citizens who are trained to fight but who only serve in time of emergency.

miner: someone who digs tunnels as part of a military operation in order to destroy the enemy's fortifications with explosives.

minority: a group of people, such as African Americans, that is smaller than or different from the larger group. Also less than half of the people or voters.

missionary: a member of a religious group that is sent into another area to spread the word about his or her religion's teachings and perform works of service.

moor: to secure a ship with anchors and lines.

mother country: the country to which people from a colony owe their allegiance.

musket: a long gun used by soldiers before the invention of the rifle.

muster out: to be discharged from the military.

mutiny: an open rebellion by soldiers or sailors against their commanding officers.

negotiate: to discuss and reach an agreement.

Nisei: a person born in the United States whose parents were immigrants from Japan.

overthrow: to forcibly remove from power.

Parliament: the law-making body of British government.

pastor: a minister of a church.

patriotism: devotion to and love for one's country.

peninsula: a piece of land that juts out into water.

persevere: to carry on doing something even in the face of great difficulty.

petition: to formally request something.

picket: to stand outside a workplace or store in protest.

plaintiff: a person who brings a case in a court of law.

port: a harbor where ships can load and unload.

poverty: having little money or few material possessions.

Glossary

prejudice: an unfair feeling of dislike for a person or group, usually based on gender, race, or religion.

principle: an important idea or belief that guides an individual or community.

propaganda: biased, misleading, or false information that is promoted to persuade people to believe a certain viewpoint.

protest: to object to something, often in public.

race: a group of people that shares distinct physical qualities, such as skin color.

racism: the belief that some races are superior to others and have the right to dominate them.

racist: hatred of people of a different race.

ration: to allow someone to have only a set amount of food or provisions.

rebel: a person who resists the rules or government of the society he or she lives in. Also to fight against authority or someone fighting against authority.

rebellion: an organized attempt to overthrow a government or other authority.

recruit: to get someone to join you or help you. Also a person who joins to help.

Redcoat: a name for British soldiers during the Revolutionary War.

redoubt: a small, enclosed fort to protect soldiers during an attack.

resistance: a force that opposes or slows down another force.

restriction: a limit on something.

revolt: to fight against a government or person of authority.

revolution: a radical, widespread change in a political or social system of a country.

Revolutionary War: the war of independence fought between America and England between 1775 and 1783.

rights: what is due to a person naturally or legally.

rumor: a story or report that is shared by many people that may or may not be true.

sabotage: the planned destruction of property, or an act that interferes with work or another activity.

salvage: to rescue a wrecked or disabled ship at sea.

sapper: a soldier responsible for building roads, fortifications, and tunnels to approach an enemy position.

schooner: a type of sailing ship with two or more masts.

Glossary

scout: a soldier sent ahead of the main group to gather information about the enemy's position and strength.

scythe: a tool that consists of a long, curved blade on a pole with two handles that is used for cutting grain crops.

segregate: laws and customs designed to keep certain groups of people isolated from each other.

shackle: to chain a prisoner's wrists or ankles together.

siege: when the military surrounds a town or enemy fort and does not allow anything in or out.

silt: particles of fine soil.

slave: a person owned by another person and forced to work without pay, against their will.

smuggle: to move goods illegally in or out of a country.

strike: when a union of workers refuse to work as a tool to get concessions from their employer.

tax: money charged by a government.

tinderbox: a box containing tinder, flint, and other items needed to light a fire.

tolerance: the willingness to accept behavior and beliefs that are different from your own.

trade: the buying, selling, or exchange of goods and services between countries.

traitor: someone who is disloyal and abandons or betrays a group or cause.

treason: actions that go against one's own country.

troops: soldiers.

union: an organized group of workers formed to protect and extend their rights and interests.

unjust: not fair.

War Relocation Authority: the government agency that handled the forced relocation and detention of Japanese Americans during World War II.

Yellow Peril: the belief in the United States in the early twentieth century that immigration from Japan and China was dangerous to the nation.

Resources

Books

Hoose, Philip. *Claudette Colvin: Twice Toward Justice*. New York: Farrar, Straus, Giroux, 2009.

Houston, Jeanne Watasuki and James D. Houston. *Farewell to Manzanar*. New York: Houghton Mifflin, 1973.

Martin, Joseph Plumb. *Private Yankee Doodle: Being a Narrative of Some of the Adventures, Dangers and Sufferings of a Revolutionary Soldier*. Eastern Acorn Press, 1962.

Murphy, Jim. *A Young Patriot: The American Revolution as Experienced by One Boy*. New York: Houghton Mifflin, 1998.

Meyers, Walter Dean. *Amistad: A Long Road to Freedom*. Dutton, 1996.

Ryan, Pam Muñoz. *Esperanza Rising*. New York: Scholastic, 2000.

Websites

History Animated
This website lets you choose from several different animated maps that move, step-by-step, through key events in the War for Independence.
historyanimated.com/verynewhistorywaranimated/?page_id=17

Mr. Nussbaum Learning + Fun
This website has several short History Channel videos that cover key events in the American Revolution.
mrnussbaum.com/amrevolution/videos

In the Shadow of My Country: A Japanese Artist Remembers
Artist Roger Shimomura illustrated the diary his grandmother kept while she was interned during World War II.
densho.org/learning/shadow/module/index.html

The Rise and Fall of Jim Crow
A website and four-part series on PBS that examines segregation after the Civil War.
pbs.org/wnet/jimcrow/index.html

Movies/Documentaries/Audio

Amistad. Steven Spielberg, director and producer. DreamWorks, 1997.

"The Farm Workers Strike, Episode V." *Latino Americans: Pride and Prejudice*. PBS, 2013.

Want to hear a speech by Dr. Martin Luther King Jr.? You can listen to it here. *youtube.com/watch?v=5TmoFoG5P-U*